500 FACTS
Science

500 FACTS
Science

First published in 2009 by Miles Kelly Publishing Ltd
Bardfield Centre, Great Bardfield, Essex, CM7 4SL

Copyright © Miles Kelly Publishing Ltd 2009

The sections in this book are also available as individual titles

2 4 6 8 10 9 7 5 3 1

Editorial Director Belinda Gallagher
Art Director Jo Brewer
Editions Manager Bethan Ellish
Cover Designer Simon Lee
Designer John Christopher (White Design)
Indexer Jane Parker
Production Manager Elizabeth Brunwin
Reprographics Stephan Davis, Jennifer Hunt, Ian Paulyn
Contributors Sue Becklake, Peter Bond, Duncan Brewer,
Clive Carpenter, Clare Oliver, Steve Parker, Peter Riley,
Dr Kristina Routh, Barbara Taylor

All images are from the Miles Kelly Archives

ISBN 978-1-84810-200-2

Printed in China

British Library Cataloguing-in-Publication Data
A catalogue record for this book is available from the British Library

Made with paper from a sustainable forest

www.mileskelly.net
info@mileskelly.net

www.factsforprojects.com
The one-stop homework helper —
pictures, facts, videos, projects and more

Contents

SCIENCE 176–217

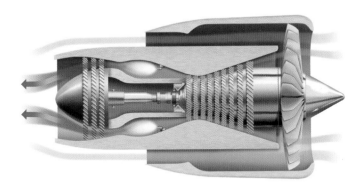

Inventors of the Stone Age

1 **Humans have always been inventors.**
Over 400,000 years ago, our ancient relatives made stone tools such as axes. Then about 30,000 years ago they discovered how to sew skins together to make clothes. Bones were first used as musical instruments over 20,000 years ago. Early people also learned how to use fire and invented cooking and ways of lighting the darkness. Because they lived by hunting animals, early humans invented bows and arrows to which they added sharp stone tips. They learned how to keep warm and dry by building shelters and homes made from tree branches, rocks and huge woolly mammoth tusks.

▶ Stone Age clothes were made out of animal skins sewn together using a bone needle.

The first tools

2 **The first inventors lived about 2.5 million years ago.** They were small, human-like creatures who walked upright on two legs. Their first inventions were stone tools. They hammered stones with other stones to shape them. These rough tools have been found in Tanzania in Africa. Scientists call this early relative of ours 'handy man'.

3 **Stone Age people made really sharp weapons and tools by chipping a stone called flint.** They dug pits and tunnels in chalky ground to find the valuable flint lumps. Their digging tools were made from reindeer antlers.

▲ Stone Age hunters trapped woolly mammoths in pits and killed them with spears.

▲ Flint tools were shaped to fit comfortably into the hand, with finely chipped cutting edges that could cut through large bones.

4 **Early hunters were able to kill the largest animals.** With flint tips on their weapons, they overcame wild oxen and horses and even killed huge, woolly mammoths. They used their sharp flint tools to carve up the bodies. The flint easily sliced through tough animal hides.

5 **The axe was a powerful weapon.** A new invention, the axe handle, made it possible to strike very hard blows. Fitted with a sharp stone head, the axe was useful for chopping down trees for firewood and building shelters.

▲ Axe heads were valuable, and were traded with people who had no flint.

I DON'T BELIEVE IT!

Some Stone Age hunters used boomerangs! They made them out of mammoth tusks thousands of years before Australian boomerangs, and used them for hunting.

6 **Saws could cut through the hardest wood.** Flint workers discovered how to make very small flint flakes. They fixed the flakes like teeth in a straight handle of wood or bone. If the teeth broke, they could fix new ones. Saws were used to cut through tough bones as well as wood.

▼ Saws were made from about 12,000 BC, and had flint 'teeth' held in place by resin.

The fire makers

7 **People once used fire created by lightning.** Discovering how to use fire made life a lot easier. The first fire users lived in Africa more than 250,000 years ago. Over thousands of years, these people spread into Europe and Asia. Winters were very cold further north. Fire helped people stay warm. They went on to discover how to twirl a fire stick very fast. This was done by placing the loop of a bowstring around the stick and moving the bow back and forth. After thousands of years, people invented a way to make sparks from steel by hitting it with a flint. Now they could carry their fire-making tinderboxes around with them.

▶ Fire provided early people with warmth, light and heat to cook food. The temperature deep within a cave stays the same whatever the weather outside.

MAKING HEAT

When your hands are cold you rub them together. Do this slowly. They feel the same. Now rub them together really fast. Feel how your hands get warmer. Rubbing things together is called friction. Friction causes heat.

8 **Fire makes food taste good.** The invention of cooking made food safer, because cooking kills germs. Cooking roots and meat on a fire makes them more tender as well as tastier. Humans are the only animals that cook food.

9 **Humans invented lamps to light deep, dark caves.** The lamps were saucers of clay or stone that burned animal fat, with moss for a wick. Campfire flames kept wild animals away at night. They also cooked food and kept people warm. People could see to make wall paintings in the caves.

New ways of moving

10 **With wheels you can move enormous weights.** Once, heavy weights were dragged along the ground, sometimes on sledges. In Scandinavia, parts of 7000-year-old sledges have been found. Over 5500 years ago, the Sumerians of Mesopotamia began to use wheels made from carved planks fastened together.

Metal rim

Plank fastening

▲ Plank wheels were very heavy, and metal rims helped hold them together.

▼ Spoked wheels made chariots light, fast and easy to steer.

11 **Warriors had light, strong wheels on their fighting chariots.** Wheels with spokes are lighter than solid plank wheels. From about 1800BC, the ancient Egyptians were using light chariots with spoked wheels. Horses pulled them fast in battle. The ancient Greeks and Romans used them for chariot races as well as for fighting.

Spoke

Light rim

Lightweight frame

Hobby (1818)

Velocipede (1861)
(Boneshaker)

Penny Farthing (early 1870s)

Mountain bike (1976)

◀ From the earliest boneshaker to today's mountain bike, the bicycle has always been popular.

12 **Railway lines were once made of wood!** Wheels move easily along rails. Horses pulled heavy wagons on these wagonways over 400 years ago. William Jessop invented specially shaped metal wheels to run along metal rails in 1789. Modern trains haul enormous loads at great speed along metal rails.

13 **In 1861, bikes with solid tyres were called boneshakers!** However, an even earlier version of the bicycle was invented by the Frenchman, Count of Sivrac, in 1790. It had no pedals and was moved by the feet pushing against the ground. The invention of air-filled rubber tyres made cycling more comfortable.

14 **Cars with gigantic wheels can drive over other cars!** Big wheels give a smooth ride. At some motor shows, trucks with enormous wheels compete to drive over rows of cars. Tractors with huge wheels were invented to drive over very rough ground.

QUIZ
WHICH CAME FIRST?

1. (a) the chariot, or (b) the sledge?
2. (a) solid wheels, or (b) spoked wheels?
3. (a) rails, or (b) steam engine?
4. (a) tyres with inner-tubes, or (b) solid tyres?
5. (a) the boneshaker, or (b) the mountain bike?

Answers:
1.b 2.a 3.a 4.b 5.a

▶ Wheels this size are usually only found on giant dump trucks. These carry heavy loads such as rocks or soil that can be tipped out.

Harvesting the earth

15 **The first farmers used digging sticks.** In the area now called Iraq, about 9000 BC, farmers broke the ground and planted seeds of wheat and barley. They used knives made of flint flakes fixed in a bone or wooden handle to cut the ripe grain stalks. The quern was an invention for grinding grain into flour between two stones.

▲ Curved knives made of bone or wood were used for harvesting grain.

I DON'T BELIEVE IT!

Some Stone Age people invented the first refrigerators! They buried spare food in pits dug in ground that was always frozen.

16 **Humans pulled the first ploughs.** They were invented in Egypt and surrounding countries as early as 4000 BC. Ploughs broke the ground and turned over the soil faster and better than digging sticks. Later on, oxen and other animals pulled ploughs. The invention of metal ploughs made ploughing much easier.

◄ Ploughed furrows made it easier to sow, water and harvest crops.

17 New inventions changed farming forever. For thousands of years farming hardly changed. Then, about 300 years ago, there were many new inventions. One of these was a seed-drill, invented by Englishman Jethro Tull. Pulled by a horse, it sowed seeds at regular spaces in neat rows. It was less wasteful than the old method of throwing grain onto the ground.

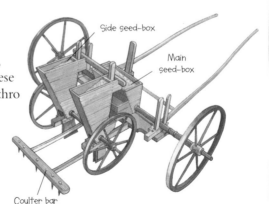

Side seed-box

Main seed-box

Coulter bar

▲ Jethro Tull's seed-drill sowed three rows of seed at a time.

18 Modern machines harvest huge fields of wheat in record time. The combine harvester was invented to cut the crop and separate grain at the same time. Teams of combine harvesters roll across America's wide plains harvesting the wheat. What were once huge areas of land covered with grass now provide the grain for America's bread.

19 Scientists are changing the way plants grow. They have invented ways of creating crop plants with built-in protection from pests and diseases. Other bumper crop plants grow well in places where once they could not grow at all because of the soil or weather.

▼ The latest combine harvesters have air-conditioned, soundproofed cabs and some even have sound systems.

Under attack!

20 **Using a spear thrower is like having an arm twice the normal length.** Spear throwers were invented about 15,000 BC. Hunters and warriors used them to hurl spears harder and farther than ever before. People all over the world invented this useful tool, and Australian Aborigines still use it.

◄ One end of the spear thrower is cupped to hold the spear butt.

▼ Bowmen often stood behind lines of sharpened stakes that protected them from enemies on horseback.

21 **Arrows from a longbow could pass through iron armour.** Bows and arrows were invented at least 20,000 years ago. More than 900 years ago, the English longbow was made from a yew branch. Archers used it to fire many arrows a long distance in a short time. By law, all Englishmen had to practise regularly with the longbow. It helped them win many famous battles.

I DON'T BELIEVE IT!

Longbow archers could aim and fire six arrows per minute. The arrow sometimes went straight through an enemy's armour and out the other side.

22 **Crossbows had to be wound up for each shot.** They were invented over 2000 years ago in the Mediterranean area, and fired a metal bolt or short arrow. They were powerful and accurate, but much slower than longbows. Soldiers used them in sieges throughout Europe from about AD 1000 onwards. But in battles, where speed was important, crossbows were often beaten by longbows.

▶ Crossbows were the first mechanical hand weapons, and at one time the Church tried to ban them.

23 **In the Bible, David killed the giant, Goliath, with a pebble from a sling.** The sling is an ancient weapon probably invented by shepherds. They used it when guarding their flocks, and still do in some countries. The slinger holds the two loose ends, and puts a pebble in the pouch. Then he whirls it round his head and lets go of one end. The pebble flies out at the target.

24 **A schoolboy's catapult can do a lot of damage.** The rubber strips are like bowstrings, which can fire a pebble from a pouch, like a sling. Some anglers use a catapult to fire food to attract fish to the water's surface.

From stone to metal

25 Sometimes pieces of pure natural gold or copper can be found in the ground. The earliest metal workers from about 8000 BC, in the eastern Mediterranean, beat these metals with stone tools. They made the first copper weapons and gold ornaments.

▶ Gold is quite soft, and early goldsmiths beat it into a variety of shapes and made patterns of hammered indentations on its surface.

26 Blowing air onto flames makes them hotter. About 8500 years ago people discovered how to melt metals out of the rocks, or ores, containing them. They invented bellows – animal-skin bags, to blow air onto the flames. The hot flames melted the metal out of the ore. We call this 'smelting' the metal.

27 Bronze weapons stay sharper for longer than copper ones. About 5500 years ago, metal workers invented bronze by smelting copper ores and tin ores together. They used the bronze to make hard, sharp swords, spearheads and axe heads.

◀ Molten bronze was poured into moulds of stone or clay to make tools.

▶ Bronze axes were sharper, and less easily damaged than stone ones.

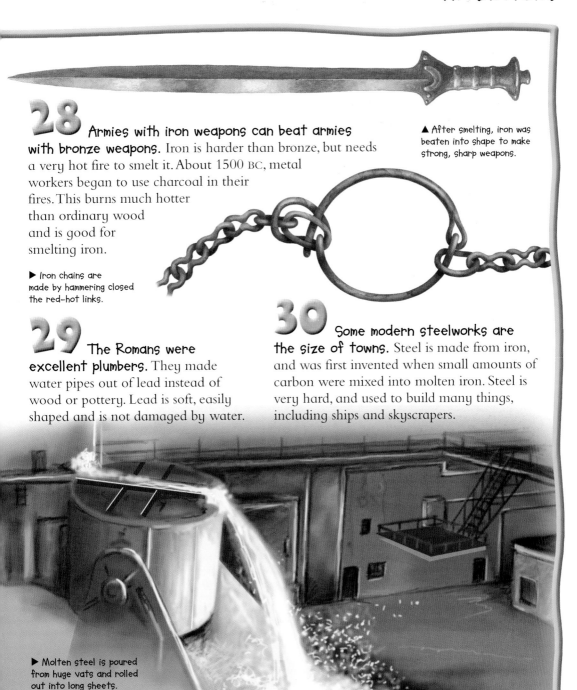

28
Armies with iron weapons can beat armies with bronze weapons. Iron is harder than bronze, but needs a very hot fire to smelt it. About 1500 BC, metal workers began to use charcoal in their fires. This burns much hotter than ordinary wood and is good for smelting iron.

▲ After smelting, iron was beaten into shape to make strong, sharp weapons.

▶ Iron chains are made by hammering closed the red-hot links.

29
The Romans were excellent plumbers. They made water pipes out of lead instead of wood or pottery. Lead is soft, easily shaped and is not damaged by water.

30
Some modern steelworks are the size of towns. Steel is made from iron, and was first invented when small amounts of carbon were mixed into molten iron. Steel is very hard, and used to build many things, including ships and skyscrapers.

▶ Molten steel is poured from huge vats and rolled out into long sheets.

Boats and sail

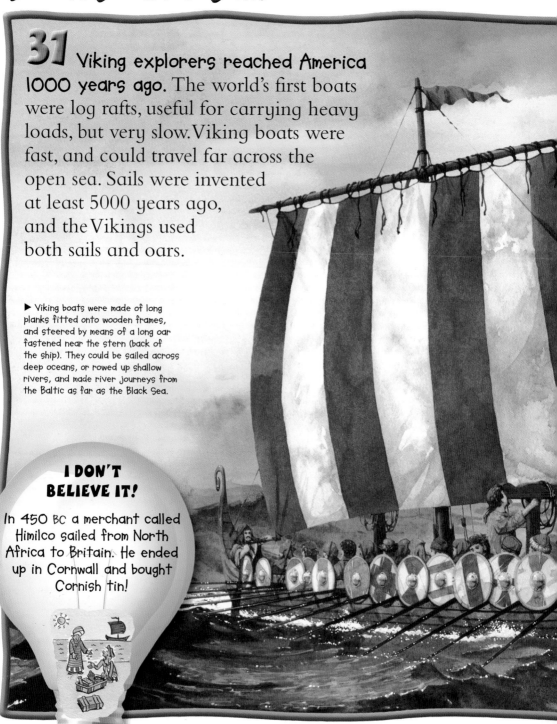

31 **Viking explorers reached America 1000 years ago.** The world's first boats were log rafts, useful for carrying heavy loads, but very slow. Viking boats were fast, and could travel far across the open sea. Sails were invented at least 5000 years ago, and the Vikings used both sails and oars.

▶ Viking boats were made of long planks fitted onto wooden frames, and steered by means of a long oar fastened near the stern (back of the ship). They could be sailed across deep oceans, or rowed up shallow rivers, and made river journeys from the Baltic as far as the Black Sea.

I DON'T BELIEVE IT!

In 450 BC a merchant called Himilco sailed from North Africa to Britain. He ended up in Cornwall and bought Cornish tin!

32 About 300 years ago sailing ships sailed all the world's oceans. Some, like the British man-of-war fighting ships, were enormous, with many sails and large crews of sailors. Countries such as Britain, France, Spain and Holland had large navies made up of these ships.

33 Some sailing boats race around the world non-stop. Modern sailing boats use many inventions, such as machines to roll up the sails and gears that allow the boat to steer itself. These boats are tough, light and very fast.

Wonderful clay

34 **Stone Age hunters used baked clay to do magic.** At least 30,000 years ago in Central Europe they discovered that some clay went hard in the sun, and even harder in a fire. They made little clay figures of animals and humans. These were probably used in magic spells to help the hunters catch food. Hardening clay in a fire was the start of the invention of pottery.

◀ Some early clay figures may have been made to represent ancestors or gods and goddesses.

▶ Kilns produced much higher temperatures than open fires, and the heat could be controlled.

35 **Hard clay bowls changed the way people ate.** The first known pots were made around 10,000 BC in Japan. They were shaped by hand and hardened in fires. They could hold liquid, and were used to boil meat and plants. This made the food tastier and more tender. Around 7000 BC, potters in Southeast Asia used a new invention – a special oven to harden and waterproof clay, called a kiln.

36 **Potters' wheels were probably invented before cart wheels.** About 3500 BC in Mesopotamia (modern Iraq), potters invented a wheel on which to turn lumps of clay and shape round pots. By spinning the clay, the potter could make smooth, perfectly round shapes quickly.

Clay pot

Heat duct

Fuel

37

Brick-making was invented in hot countries without many trees. The first brick buildings were built in 9000 BC in the Jordan Valley. House builders made bricks from clay and straw, and dried them in the hot sun. By 3500 BC, bricks hardened in kilns were used in important buildings in Mesopotamia.

▶ With the invention of bricks, it was possible to construct large buildings. In 6000 BC, the Turkish town of Çatal Hüyük had houses with rooftop openings connected by ladders instead of doors.

Flat roof

Trap door

Ladder

Roof beams

38

Modern factories make thousands of pots at a time. They are 'fired' in huge kilns. Wheels with electric motors are used, though much factory pottery is shaped in moulds. Teams of workers paint patterns.

▼ Decorating pottery by hand and reproducing the pattern accurately requires much skill.

MAKE A COILED POT

Roll modelling clay into a long, 'snake' shape. Coil some of it into a flat circle. Continue to coil, building the coils upward. Try and make a bowl shape, and finally smooth out the ridges.

Sailing into the unknown

39 **Early sailors looked at the stars to find their way about.** Around 1000 BC, Phoenician merchants from Syria were able to sail out of sight of land without getting lost. They knew in which direction certain stars lay. The north Pole Star, in the Little Bear constellation (star group), always appears in the north.

▲ Two stars in the Great Bear constellation are called the Pointers. They point to the north Pole Star in the Little Bear constellation.

40 **Magnetic compasses always point north and south.** They allow sailors to navigate (find their way) even when the stars are invisible. The Chinese invented the magnetic compass about 3000 years ago. It was first used in Europe about 1000 years ago.

► Compasses have a magnetized needle placed on a pivot so it can turn easily. Beneath this is a card with marked points to show direction.

► Using stick and shell maps, Pacific islanders successfully crossed thousands of kilometres of ocean.

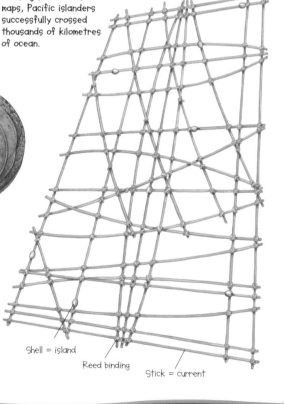

41 **Early maps showed where sea monsters lived.** The first world map was drawn by the Greek Ptolemy in AD 160. Greek maps of around 550 BC showed the known world surrounded by water in which monsters lived. Over 500 years ago, Pacific islanders had maps of sticks and shells, showing islands and currents. The first globe was invented in 1492 by a German, Martin Behain.

Shell = island

Reed binding

Stick = current

▼ The chronometer was invented by Englishman John Harrison in 1735. It was a reliable timepiece, specially mounted to remove the effect of a ship's motion at sea.

Mirrors

Telescope

▶ The sextant was developed in the mid-1700s and was an important navigation aid until the 1900s.

Moving arm

Scale

42 Eighteenth-century sailors could work out exactly where they were on the oceans. They used an instrument called a sextant, invented in 1731. The sextant measured the height of the Sun from the horizon. The chronometer was an extremely reliable clock that wasn't affected by the motion of the sea.

USING A COMPASS

Take a compass outside and find out which direction is north. Put a cardboard arrow with 'N' on it on the ground pointing in the right direction. Then try to work out the directions of south, west and east.

43 New direction-finding inventions can tell anyone exactly where they are. A hand-held instrument, called a GPS receiver, receives signals from satellites in space. It shows your position within a few metres. These receivers can be built into cars, ships, planes – even laptop computers!

Satellite orbit

Global Positioning Satellite (GPS)

◀ Modern navigation instruments use signals from several satellites to pinpoint their position.

Weapons of war

I DON'T BELIEVE IT!

In 1453 the biggest cannon in the world could fire a half-tonne cannon ball for a mile. It was used by the Turkish Sultan Mehmet to win the siege of Constantinople.

44 **The Romans invented massive rock-hurling weapons.** In medieval times, armies in Europe and the Middle East still used the same weapons in city and castle sieges. The trebuchet slung great rocks or burning material over city walls. The ballista fired missiles such as stones or spears with huge force at the enemy.

45 **The first gunpowder was used in fireworks.** The Chinese invented gunpowder over 1000 years ago. In 1221 they used it to make exploding bombs and in 1288 they invented the first gun, a cannon. Cannons and mortars, which fired bombs or large stone balls very high through the air, were used in European sieges from the 14th century onwards. The first small firearms carried by soldiers appeared in the 15th century.

46 **The battering ram could smash through massive city walls and gates.** The Egyptians may have invented it in 2000 BC to destroy brick walls. It was a huge tree-trunk, often with an iron head, swung back and forth in a frame. Sometimes it had a roof to protect the soldiers from rocks and arrows from above.

Siege tower

Ballista

▶ Medieval sieges of well-protected forts or cities sometimes lasted for months.

47 **Greek fire was a secret weapon that burned in water.** The Greeks invented it in the 7th century AD to destroy ships attacking Constantinople. A chemical mixture was squirted at enemies through copper pipes. It was still being used many centuries later in medieval sieges, pumped down onto the heads of attackers.

▲ The Gatling gun could fire six bullets a second.

48 **Gunpowder was used in tunnels to blow up castle walls.** Attackers in a siege dug tunnels under the walls and supported them with wooden props. Then, they blew up or burned away the props so that the walls collapsed.

49 **Modern machine guns can fire thousands of bullets per minute.** Richard Gatling, an American, invented the first machine gun in 1862. As in all modern guns, each machine-gun bullet has its own metal case packed with deadly explosives.

Trebuchet

Battering ram

Measuring time

50 The huge stone slabs of Stonehenge can be used as a calendar. Some of its stones are lined up with sunrise on the longest day of the year. It was built and rebuilt in Wiltshire in southern England between 3000 BC and 1550 BC.

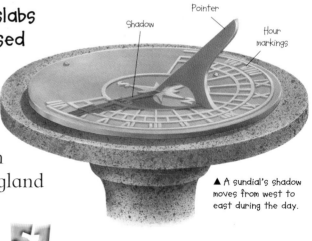

Pointer

Shadow

Hour markings

▲ A sundial's shadow moves from west to east during the day.

▼ Raising the huge main stones of Stonehenge required the muscles of many workers and the know-how of skilled Bronze Age engineers.

51 One of the earliest clocks was a stick stuck in the ground. Invented in Egypt up to 4000 years ago, the length of the shadow showed the time of day. Later sundials had a face marked with hours, and a pointer that cast a shadow.

52

Candles, water and sand can all be used to tell the time. The Egyptians invented a clock that dripped water at a fixed rate about 1400 BC. Candle clocks were marked with rings, and in the hourglass, invented about AD 1300, sand ran between two glass globes.

▼ ▶ A candle clock (below) and an hourglass (right) show a time period has passed, not the time of day.

▼ Until the invention of quartz movements, wristwatches contained springs and cogs.

Winder

Main spring   Gear wheel   Ratchet wheel

53

You can't see any moving parts in a modern quartz clock. Early clocks depended on movement. A Dutchman, Christiaan Huygens, invented a clock in 1656 which depended on a swinging pendulum. About the same time, clocks driven by coiled springs were invented. Modern quartz crystal clocks work on invisible vibrations and are very accurate. They were first produced in 1929.

▶ Wrist watches were not made until 1790. Many modern watches have a liquid crystal display (LCD) and show changing numerals instead of hour and minute hands.

MAKE A SHADOW CLOCK

Fix about 60 centimetres of garden cane upright in a flat piece of ground. Use lollipop sticks or twigs to mark the length of the shadow every hour, from 9 a.m. to 4 p.m. if possible. Which hour casts the shortest shadow?

Answer:
12 o'clock midday

54

Some clocks are like toys. Swiss cuckoo clocks contain a bird on a spring that flies out of a little door and 'cuckoos' the time. Some 18th-century clocks looked like ships, and their guns fired to mark the hours.

Harvesting nature's energy

55 **The first inventions to use wind-power were sailing boats.** Invented around 3500 BC by the Egyptians, and also by the Sumerians of Mesopotamia, the first sailing boats had a single square sail. By AD 600, windmills for grinding grain had been invented in Arab countries. Some European windmills, in use from about AD 1100 onwards, could be turned to face the wind.

56 **The first waterwheels invented were flat, not upright.** Used around 100 BC in Yugoslavia and Albania, they needed very fast streams to drive them. One century later, Roman upright waterwheels worked better and had gears to slow them down. As well as grinding corn, some were used to drive pumps or saws.

Direction vane

Sail

Main drive

Angled gears

Vertical Shaft

Millstones

Flour chute

► Many windmills were made entirely of wood apart from the millstones.

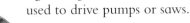
◀ In overshot watermills, the water strikes the top of the millwheel.

▶ Trevithick's locomotive used high-pressure steam, and he demonstrated it in 1808 on a circular track in London, at speeds of up to 16 kilometres an hour.

57 **Early steam engines often threatened to explode.** Thomas Savery's 1698 steam pump, invented in Devon, England, wasted fuel and was dangerous. Englishman Richard Trevithick developed a steam engine to move on tracks in 1804.

58 **Spinning magnets can create an electric current.** Michael Faraday and other scientists invented the first magnetic electricity generators (producers) in the 1830s. Today, huge dams use the power of millions of tonnes of flowing water to turn electricity generating machinery. They still use moving magnets to make electricity.

59 **The strength of the wind usually increases the higher up you are.** Some of the largest wind turbines in use today stand as high as a 20-storey building, with propellers spanning more than the length of a football pitch. They produce enough electricity to power 1400 homes or more.

I DON'T BELIEVE IT!

The earliest steam engine was totally useless. A 3rd century BC Greek engineer invented a steam machine with a spinning metal ball. Unfortunately no one could think of any use for it.

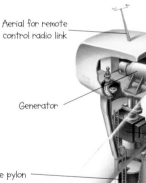

Aerial for remote control radio link

Rotor Blade

Generator

Transformer

Stairs inside pylon

◀ An increasing number of wind turbines are being built to make electricity.

Marks on a page

Phoenician

Classical Greek

Roman

A B C D E F

Cyrillic

А Б В Г Д Е

Modern Hebrew

Modern Arabic

Ancient Egyptian

Chinese

人 月 子 水 雨 木

Japanese

星 面 海 水 下

▲ Ancient picture writing used hundreds of different signs, but most modern alphabets have far fewer letters.

60 **The first writing was made up of pictures.** Writing was invented by the Sumerians 5500 years ago. They scratched their writing onto clay tablets. The most famous word pictures are the 'hieroglyphs' of ancient Egyptians from about 5000 years ago. Cuneiform writing was made up of wedge shapes pressed into clay with a reed. It followed the Sumerian picture writing.

▲ Some of the religious books handwritten by monks were decorated with beautiful illustrations.

61 **The world's first book was a roll of paper made from reeds.** It was produced in Egypt between 1500 BC and 1350 BC and was called 'The Book of the Dead'. Christian monks used to write their religious books on sheets of parchment made from animal skins.

62 Reading suddenly became much more popular after the invention of printing. A German, John Gutenberg, was an early inventor of a printing press with movable letters in the 15th century. By the end of the century there were printing presses all over Europe.

▲ The first printing presses were made of wood, and used movable wooden letters.

63 Once, people were expert at doing sums on their fingers. The first written numbers were invented about 3100 BC by Middle Eastern traders. Around AD 300, the Chinese invented a counting machine called an abacus. It was a frame with beads strung on wires. Some people still use them.

▶ Experts can do complicated sums very fast on an abacus.

I DON'T BELIEVE IT!

Some early Greek writing was called, 'the way an ox ploughs the ground'. It was written from right to left, then the next line went left to right, and so on, back and forth.

64 Computers do sums at lightning speed. Early modern computers were invented in the United States and Europe in the 1930s and 1940s. Today, computers are small, cheap and extremely powerful. They can store whole libraries of information. The Internet allows everyone to share information and send email messages immediately almost anywhere in the world.

Making things bigger

65 **Small pieces of glass can make everything look bigger.** Spectacle-makers in Italy in the 14th century made their own glass lenses to look through. These helped people to read small writing. Scientists later used these lenses to invent microscopes, to see very small things, and telescopes, to see things far away.

▲ Spectacles became important as more people began to read books.

66 **Scientists saw the tiny bacteria that cause illness for the first time with microscopes.** The Dutch invented the first microscopes, which had one lens. In the 1590s Zacharias Janssen of Holland invented the first microscope with two lenses, which was much more powerful.

67 **The Dutch tried to keep the first telescope a secret.** Hans Lippershey invented it in 1608, but news soon got out. Galileo, an Italian scientist, built one in 1609. He used it to get a close look at the Moon and the planets.

▲ Early microscopes with two or more lenses, like those of English inventor Robert Hooke (1635–1703), were powerful, but the image was unclear.

QUIZ

1. Are lenses made from (a) glass, or (b) steel?

2. Which came first, (a) the telescope, or (b) spectacles?

3. Do you study stars with (a) a microscope, or (b) a telescope?

4. Which are smaller, (a) bacteria, or (b) ants

5. Do modern microscopes make things look, (a) hundreds of times bigger, or (b) thousands of times bigger?

Answers:
1.a 2.b 3.b 4.a 5.b

68 You cannot look through a radio telescope. An American, Grote Reber, invented the first one and built it in his backyard in 1937. Radio telescopes pick up radio signals from space with a dish-shaped receiver. The signals come from distant stars, and, more recently, from space probes.

▲ Telescopes changed the mistaken idea that the Universe revolved around the Earth.

▼ An electron microscope can magnify a mosquito to monster size, and reveal tiny creatures that are normally invisible.

▲ Most radio telescope dishes can be moved to face in any direction.

69 Modern microscopes make things look thousands of times bigger. A German, Ernst Ruska, invented the first electron microscope in 1933. It made things look 12,000 times their actual size. The latest microscopes can magnify things millions of times.

37

Making music

70 **Humans are the only animals that play tunes on musical instruments.** Stone Age people invented rattles and other noise-makers, and made them from mammoth bones and tusks. Instruments you hit or rattle are called percussion instruments. They are still used in modern orchestras.

71 **Over 20,000 years ago Stone Age Europeans invented whistles and flutes.** They made them out of bones or antlers. Modern flutes still work in a similar way, by covering and uncovering holes in a tube while blowing down it.

72 **Some of the earliest harps invented were made from the shells of tortoises.** The first harps were played in Sumeria and Egypt about 5000 years ago. Modern harps, like most ancient harps, have strings of different lengths.

▼ The instruments of the modern orchestra are grouped in several sections and include the violin in the string section, the bassoon in the woodwind section and the trombone in the brass section.

Percussion

Bassoon (woodwind section)

Trombone (brass section)

73 **Pianos have padded hammers inside, which strike the strings.** The first piano-like instrument was invented in about 1480 and its strings were plucked when the keys were pressed, not struck. It made a softer sound than a modern piano.

▶ The grand piano's strings are laid out horizontally in a harp-shaped frame.

74 **The trumpet is one of the loudest instruments in the orchestra.** A trumpet was found in Tutankhamen's tomb in Egypt dating back to 1320 BC. Over 2000 years ago, Celtic warriors in northern Europe blew great bronze trumpets shaped like mammoth tusks to frighten their enemies.

75 **Bagpipes sound as strange as they look.** They were invented in India over 2000 years ago. The Roman army had bagpipe players. In the Middle Ages, European and Middle Eastern herdsmen sometimes played bagpipes while they looked after their animals.

Conductor

Violin
(string section)

Keeping in touch

76 Some African tribes used to use 'talking drums' to send messages. Native Americans used smoke signals, visible several miles away. Before electrical inventions such as the telephone, sending long-distance messages had to be a simple process.

◄ Smoke from burning vegetation could be broken up into signals by lowering and raising a blanket over the smoke.

▼ Each position of the semaphore signaller's arms forms a different letter. What does this message say?

77 Wooden arms on tall poles across the country sent signals hundreds of miles in 18th-century France. Claude Chappe invented this system, now called semaphore, in 1797. Until recently, navies used semaphore flags to signal from ship to ship. In 1838 American Samuel Morse invented a code of short and long bursts of electric current or light, called dots and dashes. It could send messages along a wire, or could be flashed with a light.

78 The telephone can send your voice around the world. A Scotsman, Alexander Graham Bell, invented it in the 1870s. When you speak, your voice is changed into electric signals that are sent along to a receiver held by the other user. Within 15 years there were 140,000 telephone owners in the United States.

1 = S
2 = I
3 = G
4 = N
5 = A
6 = L

79

Radio signals fly through the air without wires. An Italian, Guglielmo Marconi, invented the radio or 'wireless' in 1899. Radio stations send signals, carried on invisible radio waves, which are received by an antenna. A Scot, John Logie Baird, invented an early TV system in 1926. TV pictures can travel through the air or along wires.

Satellite

TV studio

TV camera

I DON'T BELIEVE IT!

Early TV performers had to wear thick, clownlike makeup. The pictures were so fuzzy that viewers could not make out their faces otherwise.

▲ Live TV images can be beamed to a satellite in space, then redirected to the other side of the world.

80

With a mobile phone you can talk to practically anyone wherever you are. Your voice is carried on radio waves called microwaves and passed from antenna to antenna until it reaches the phone you are calling. Some of the antennaes are on space satellites.

Taking to the skies

81 The first hot-air balloon passengers were a sheep, a duck and a cockerel. The French Montgolfier brothers invented the hot-air balloon in 1782. The first human passengers often had to put out fires, as the balloon was inflated by hot air created by burning straw and wool!

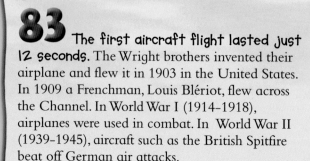

▲ The Montgolfier hot-air balloon made the first untethered, manned flight from Paris in 1783.

82 Many inventors have tried to fly by flapping birdlike wings. All have failed. One of the first bird-men crashed to his death at a Roman festival in the 1st century AD.

83 The first aircraft flight lasted just 12 seconds. The Wright brothers invented their airplane and flew it in 1903 in the United States. In 1909 a Frenchman, Louis Blériot, flew across the Channel. In World War I (1914–1918), airplanes were used in combat. In World War II (1939–1945), aircraft such as the British Spitfire beat off German air attacks.

▲ Formed in 1965, the Royal Air Force Aerobatic Team, known as the Red Arrows, uses Hawk jets. They need perfect timing to perform their close formation flying and aerobatics at high speed.

84 The first model helicopter was made by Leonardo da Vinci as long ago as 1480. In 1877, an Italian, Enrico Forlanini, invented a steam helicopter which flew for 60 seconds and reached a height of 15 metres. Modern helicopters can hover and land almost anywhere and are often used for rescue missions at land and sea.

85 In 1948 a jet plane flew faster than the speed of sound. Englishman Frank Whittle invented the first jet engine in 1930. Most modern aircraft are jets without propellers. Teams of jets, like the Red Arrows, often perform stunts at air shows.

I DON'T BELIEVE IT!

In 1783 the first hydrogen balloon was attacked and destroyed by terrified farm workers when it landed. It had flown 24 kilometres.

Keeping a record

86 **The first sound recording was the nursery rhyme, 'Mary had a little lamb'.** In 1877 an American, Thomas Edison, invented a way of recording sounds by causing a needle to scratch marks on a cylinder or tube. Moving the needle over the marks again repeated the sounds. Performers spoke or sang into a horn, and the sounds were also played back through it.

▲ Thomas Edison produced many important inventions, including sound recording, electric light bulbs and an early film-viewing machine.

87 **To play the first disc records, you had to keep turning a handle.** Emile Berlin, a German, invented disc recording in 1887. The discs were played with steel needles, and soon wore out. They also broke easily if you dropped them. Long-playing discs appeared in 1948. They had 20 minutes of sound on each side and were made of bendy plastic, which didn't break so easily.

▼ Early record players had to be wound up between records, and the loudspeaker was a large horn.

QUIZ

1. Were the first recordings on (a) discs, or (b) cylinders?
2. Which came first, (a) movies, or (b) long-playing records?
3. Was the first photograph of (a) flowers, or (b) rooftops?
4. The first movies were viewed through a hole in a box – true or false?
5. Were the first movies shown in (a) the 19th century, or (b) the 20th century?

Answers:
1.b 2.a 3.b 4.True 5.a

88 It took eight hours to take the world's first photograph in 1826. Frenchman Joseph Nicéphore Niépce was the inventor, and the first photograph was of rooftops. Early cameras were huge, and the photos were on glass plates. In 1889 American George Eastman invented rolls of film, making photography much easier.

▲ Modern digital cameras have a display that shows the view the lens sees, which is the image that will be stored.

89 The forerunner of the iPod/MP3 player was the portable laser-based CD player. It was more than ten times bigger and heavier than an iPod. Moving it often made the compact disc (CD) skip.

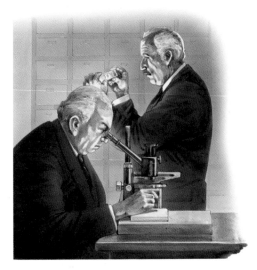

▲ The Lumière brothers, who invented the movie projector, also made films and opened the first public cinema.

▶ Launched in 2001, the iPod took little more than one year to develop.

90 Only one person at a time could watch the first movies. The viewer peered through a hole in a box. Thomas Edison's company invented movies in 1888. The invention of a projector in 1895 by the French Lumière brothers allowed a whole audience to watch the film on a screen.

Round the house

91 **A horse and cart were needed to move the first successful vacuum cleaner around.** An English engineer, Hubert Cecil Booth, invented it in 1902. The first 'Hoover' electric vacuum cleaner was built from a wooden box, an electric fan and an old sack in 1907 in America.

▼ Refrigerators were once large, noisy and had little food space.

▲ The first vacuum cleaners worked by opening and closing a bellows with a handle.

92 **Early refrigerators, invented in the 19th century, killed many people.** They leaked the poisonous gas that was used to cool them. In 1929 the gas was changed to a non-poisonous one called freon. We now know that freon causes damage to the planet's atmosphere, so that is being changed too.

QUIZ

1. Did the first 'Hoover' need (a) a horse, or (b) an electric fan?

2. Were early refrigerators dangerous because (a) they blew up or (b) they leaked poison gas?

3. The Cretans had china toilets 4000 years ago — true or false?

4. Do light bulbs contain (a) water, (b) air, or (c) neither?

5. Who opened the first electric light company, (a) Thomas Twyford, or (b) Thomas Edison?

93 A melted chocolate bar led to the invention of the microwave oven. An American, Percy L. Spencer, invented it in 1953 after noticing that a microwave machine where he worked had melted the chocolate in his pocket. In a microwave oven the microwaves make the food heat itself up from the inside. Eggs may explode because of this.

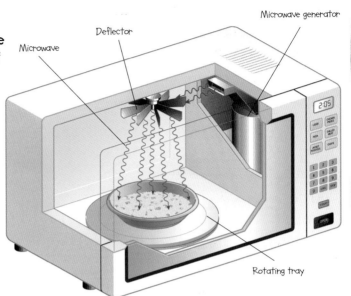

Microwave generator

Deflector

Microwave

2:05

Rotating tray

▲ In a microwave oven the microwaves are deflected by metal vanes down onto the food below.

94 There is no air inside a light bulb. If there was, it would burn out in no time. The first light bulbs failed because air could get in. American Thomas Edison invented an air-tight light bulb in 1879 that could burn for a long time. He opened the first electric light company in 1882.

Vacuum bulb

Filament

Screw thread

▶ In a light bulb, electricity causes a wire filament to glow brightly in the airless bulb.

Power contact

95 Four thousand years ago in Crete in Greece the king's palaces had flushing toilets. They used rainwater. In England, toilets that flushed when you pulled a handle were invented in the 18th century. In 1885 Thomas Twyford invented the first all-china flushing toilet.

From Earth into space

96 **Concorde flew at twice the speed of sound, nearly 2150 kilometres an hour.** This is at least twice as fast as the earliest jets. The huge jet airliner crossed the Atlantic at a height of over 18,000 metres.

◄ Concorde carried hundreds of passengers in luxury across the Atlantic in a fraction of the usual air crossing time – under 3 hours.

97 **Rockets helped the Chinese drive away a Mongol army in the 13th century.** The rockets used gunpowder, which the Chinese had invented 300 years earlier, but had only used in fireworks.

I DON'T BELIEVE IT!

A 15th-century Chinaman, Wan Hu, tried to make a flying machine out of 47 rockets and two kites. His servants lit all the rockets at the same time, and Wan Hu disappeared forever in a massive explosion.

◄ The Chinese were the first to use gunpowder in war, as in this hand-held gun for firing missiles.

98 **German war rockets in World War II could travel 321 kilometres to hit England.** They were invented by a scientist called Werner von Braun. After the war he helped the United States build space rockets.

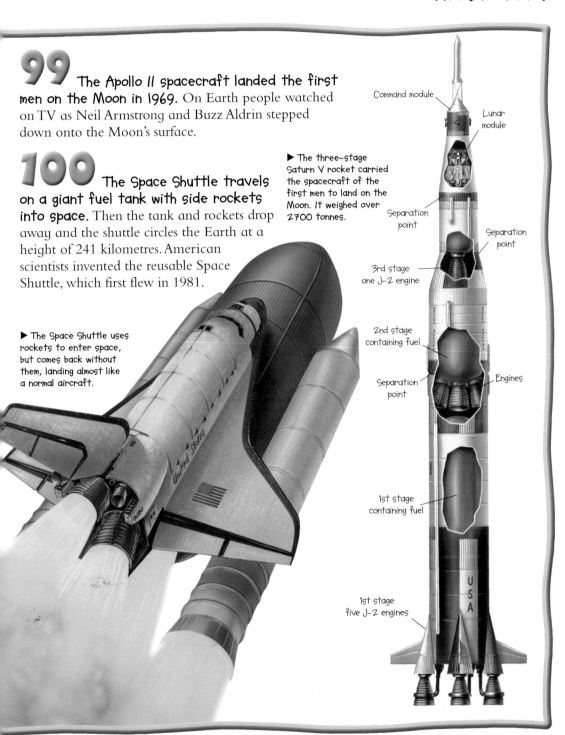

99 The Apollo II spacecraft landed the first men on the Moon in 1969. On Earth people watched on TV as Neil Armstrong and Buzz Aldrin stepped down onto the Moon's surface.

100 The Space Shuttle travels on a giant fuel tank with side rockets into space. Then the tank and rockets drop away and the shuttle circles the Earth at a height of 241 kilometres. American scientists invented the reusable Space Shuttle, which first flew in 1981.

▶ The Space Shuttle uses rockets to enter space, but comes back without them, landing almost like a normal aircraft.

Command module

Lunar module

▶ The three-stage Saturn V rocket carried the spacecraft of the first men to land on the Moon. It weighed over 2700 tonnes.

Separation point

Separation point

3rd stage one J-2 engine

2nd stage containing fuel

Separation point

Engines

1st stage containing fuel

USA

1st stage five J-2 engines

Surrounded by space

101 **Space is all around the Earth, high above the air.** Here on the Earth's surface we are surrounded by air. If you go upwards, up a mountain or in an aircraft, the air grows thinner until there is none at all. This is where space begins. Space itself is mostly empty but there are many exciting things out there such as planets, stars and galaxies. People who travel in space are called astronauts.

▶ In space, astronauts wear spacesuits to go outside the space shuttle as it circles the Earth. Much farther away are planets, stars and galaxies.

Our life-giving star

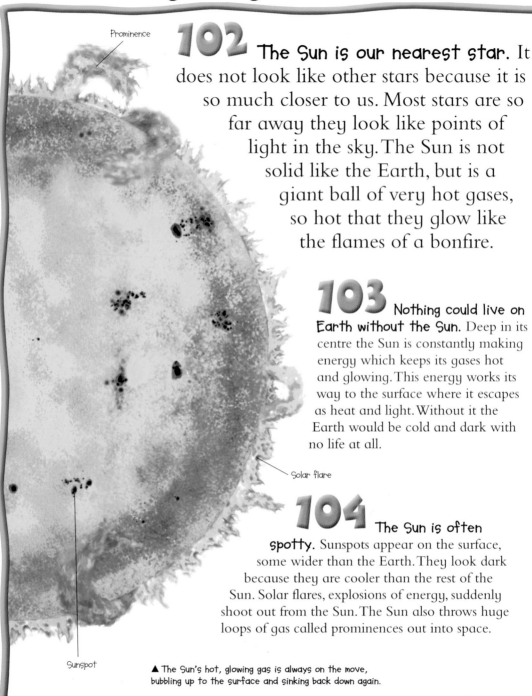

Prominence

102 **The Sun is our nearest star.** It does not look like other stars because it is so much closer to us. Most stars are so far away they look like points of light in the sky. The Sun is not solid like the Earth, but is a giant ball of very hot gases, so hot that they glow like the flames of a bonfire.

103 **Nothing could live on Earth without the Sun.** Deep in its centre the Sun is constantly making energy which keeps its gases hot and glowing. This energy works its way to the surface where it escapes as heat and light. Without it the Earth would be cold and dark with no life at all.

Solar flare

104 **The Sun is often spotty.** Sunspots appear on the surface, some wider than the Earth. They look dark because they are cooler than the rest of the Sun. Solar flares, explosions of energy, suddenly shoot out from the Sun. The Sun also throws huge loops of gas called prominences out into space.

Sunspot

▲ The Sun's hot, glowing gas is always on the move, bubbling up to the surface and sinking back down again.

105

When the Moon hides the Sun there is an eclipse. Every so often, the Sun, Moon and Earth line up in space so that the Moon comes directly between the Earth and the Sun. This stops the sunlight from reaching a small area on Earth. This area grows dark and cold, as if night has come early.

▼ When the Moon casts a shadow on the Earth, there is an eclipse of the Sun.

▶ When there is an eclipse, we can see the corona (glowing gas) around the Sun.

> ## WARNING:
> Never look directly at the Sun especially through a telescope or binoculars. It is so bright it will harm your eyes or even make you blind.

Sun

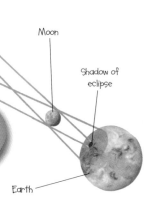

Moon

Shadow of eclipse

Earth

I DON'T BELIEVE IT!

The surface of the Sun is nearly 60 times hotter than boiling water. It is so hot it would melt a spacecraft flying near it.

A family of planets

106 **The Sun is surrounded by a family of circling planets called the Solar System.** This family is held together by an invisible force called gravity, which pulls things towards each other. It is the same force that pulls us down to the ground and stops us from floating away. The Sun's gravity pulls on the planets and keeps them circling around it.

107 **The Earth is one of eight planets in the Sun's family.** They all circle the Sun at different distances from it. The four planets nearest to the Sun are all balls of rock. The next four planets are much bigger and are made of gas and liquid. The tiny dwarf planet at the edge of the Solar System, Pluto, is a solid, icy ball.

108 **Moons circle the planets, travelling with them round the Sun.** Earth has one Moon. It circles the Earth while the Earth circles round the Sun. Dwarf planet. Mars has two tiny moons but Mercury and Venus have none at all. There are large families of moons, like miniature solar systems, around all the large gas planets.

Saturn

Uranus

Neptune

Pluto, dwarf planet

Sun

Mercury

Moon

Jupiter

Earth

Venus

Mars

▲ The eight planets are all different. Mercury, nearest the Sun, is small and hot. Then Venus, Earth and Mars are rocky and cooler. Beyond them Jupiter, Saturn, Uranus and Neptune are large and cold. Dwarf planet Pluto is tiny and icy.

109 There are millions of smaller members in the Sun's family. Some are tiny specks of dust speeding through space between the planets. Larger chunks of rock, many as large as mountains, are called asteroids. Comets come from the edge of the Solar System, skimming past the Sun before they disappear again.

I DON'T BELIEVE IT !

If the Sun was the size of a large beach ball, the Earth would be as small as a pea, and the Moon would look like a pinhead.

Planet of life

110 **The planet we live on is the Earth.** It is a round ball of rock. On the outside where we live the rock is hard and solid. But deep below our feet, inside the Earth, the rock is hot enough to melt. You can sometimes see this hot rock showering out of an erupting volcano.

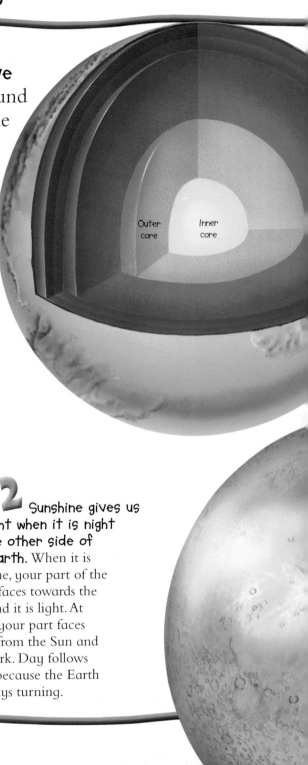

Outer core

Inner core

▶ The inner core at the centre of the Earth is made of iron. It is very hot and keeps the outer core as liquid. Outside this is the mantle, made of thick rock. The thin surface layer that we live on is called the crust.

111 **The Earth is the only planet with living creatures.** From space the Earth is a blue and white planet, with huge oceans and wet masses of cloud. People, animals and plants can live on Earth because of all this water.

112 **Sunshine gives us daylight when it is night on the other side of the Earth.** When it is daytime, your part of the Earth faces towards the Sun and it is light. At night, your part faces away from the Sun and it is dark. Day follows night because the Earth is always turning.

Crust

Mantle

I DON'T BELIEVE IT!

The Moon has no air or water. When astronauts went to the Moon they had to take air with them in their spacecraft and space suits.

New Moon

Crescent Moon

First quarter Moon

Gibbous Moon

Full Moon

113 Look for the Moon on clear nights and watch how it seems to change shape. Over a month it changes from a thin crescent to a round shape. This is because sunlight is reflected by the Moon. We see the full Moon when the sunlit side faces the Earth and a thin, crescent shape when the sunlit side is facing away from us.

114 Craters on the Moon are scars from space rocks crashing into the surface. When a rock smashes into the Moon at high speed, it leaves a saucer-shaped dent, pushing some of the rock outwards into a ring of mountains.

The Earth's neighbours

115 Venus and Mars are the nearest planets to the Earth. Venus is closer to the Sun than the Earth while Mars is farther away. Each takes a different amount of time to circle the Sun and we call this its year. A year on Venus is 225 days, on Earth 365 days and on Mars 687 days.

▲ All we can see of Venus from space are the tops of its clouds. They take just four days to race right around the planet.

116 Venus is the hottest planet. It is hotter than Mercury, although Mercury is closer to the Sun and gets more of the Sun's heat. Heat builds up on Venus because it is completely covered by clouds which trap the heat, like the glass in a greenhouse.

117 Venus has poisonous clouds with drops of acid that would burn your skin. They are not like clouds on Earth, which are made of droplets of water. These thick clouds do not let much sunshine reach the surface of Venus.

▼ Under its clouds, Venus has hundreds of volcanoes, large and small, all over its surface. We do not know if any of them are still erupting.

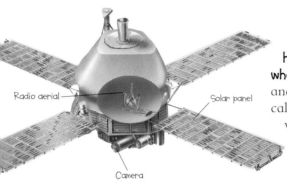

Radio aerial

Solar panel

Camera

119 Winds on Mars whip up huge dust storms that can cover the whole planet. Mars is very dry, like a desert, and covered in red dust. When a space probe called *Mariner 9* arrived there in 1971, the whole planet was hidden by dust clouds.

◀ *Mariner 9* was the first space probe to circle another planet. It sent back over 7000 pictures of Mars showing giant volcanoes, valleys, ice caps and dried-up river beds.

118 Mars has the largest volcano in the Solar System. It is called Olympus Mons and is three times as high as Mount Everest, the tallest mountain on Earth. Olympus Mons is an old volcano and it has not erupted for millions of years.

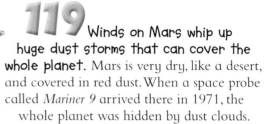

PLANET-SPOTTING

See if you can spot Venus in the night sky. It is often the first bright 'star' to appear in the evening, just above where the Sun has set. Because of this we sometimes call it the 'evening star'.

Olympus Mons

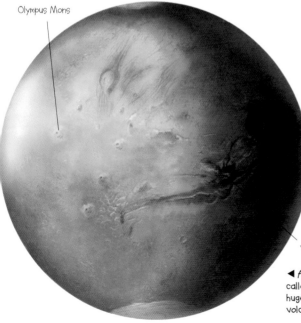

120 There are plans to send astronauts to Mars but the journey would take six months or more. The astronauts would have to take with them everything they need for the journey there and back and for their stay on Mars.

Valles Marineris

◀ An enormous valley seems to cut Mars in half. It is called Valles Marineris. To the left is a row of three huge volcanoes and beyond them you can see the largest volcano, Olympus Mons.

The smallest of all

121 Tiny Pluto is so far away, it was not discovered until 1930. In 2006, Pluto was classed as a dwarf planet. It is less than half the width of the next smallest planet, Mercury. In fact Pluto is smaller than our Moon.

▲ Pluto is too far away to see any detail on its surface, but it might look like this.

122 Dwarf planet Pluto is the farthest planet from the Sun. If you were to stand on its surface, the Sun would not look much brighter than the other stars. It gets very little heat from the Sun and its surface is completely covered with solid ice.

123 Space probes have not yet visited Pluto. So astronomers will have to wait for close-up pictures and detailed information that a probe could send back. Even if one was sent to Pluto it would take at least eight years to travel there.

124 No one knew Pluto had a moon until 1978. An astronomer noticed what looked like a bulge on the side of the planet. It turned out to be a moon and was named Charon. Charon is about half the width of Pluto.

▼ If you were on Pluto, its moon Charon would look much larger than our Moon does, because Charon is very close to Pluto.

125 Mercury looks like our Moon.

It is a round, cratered ball of rock. Although a little larger than the Moon, like the Moon it has no air.

▼ Mercury's many craters show how often it was hit by space rocks. One was so large that it shattered rocks on the other side of the planet.

MAKE CRATERS

You will need:
flour   baking tray
a marble or a stone

Spread some flour about 2 centimetres deep in a baking tray and smooth over the surface. Drop a marble or a small round stone onto the flour and see the saucer-shaped crater that it makes.

126 The sunny side of Mercury is boiling hot but the night side is freezing cold.

Being the nearest planet to the Sun the sunny side can get twice as hot as an oven. But Mercury spins round slowly so the night side has time to cool down, and there is no air to trap the heat. The night side becomes more than twice as cold as the coldest place on Earth – Antarctica.

▼ The Sun looks huge as it rises on Mercury. A traveller to Mercury would have to keep out of its heat.

The biggest of all

127 Jupiter is the biggest planet, more massive than all the other planets in the Solar System put together. It is 11 times as wide as the Earth although it is still much smaller than the Sun. Saturn, the next largest planet, is more than nine times as wide as the Earth.

Jupiter

128 Jupiter and Saturn are gas giants. They have no solid surface for a spacecraft to land on. All that you can see are the tops of their clouds. Beneath the clouds, the planets are made mostly of gas (like air) and liquid (water is a liquid).

129

The Great Red Spot on Jupiter is a 300-year-old storm. It was first noticed about 300 years ago and is at least twice as wide as the Earth. It rises above the rest of the clouds and swirls around like storm clouds on Earth.

▼ Jupiter's fast winds blow the clouds into coloured bands around the planet.

▼ There are many storms on Jupiter but none as large or long lasting as the Great Red Spot.

▼ Jupiter's Moon Io is always changing because its many volcanoes throw out new material from deep inside it.

▶ Although Saturn's rings are very wide, they stretch out in a very thin layer around the planet.

130
The shining rings around Saturn are made of millions of chunks of ice. These circle around the planet like tiny moons and shine by reflecting sunlight from their surfaces. Some are as small as ice cubes while others can be as large as a car.

131
Jupiter and Saturn spin round so fast that they bulge out in the middle. This can happen because they are not made of solid rock. As they spin their clouds are stretched out into light and dark bands around them.

I DON'T BELIEVE IT!
Saturn is the lightest planet in the Solar System. If there was a large enough sea, it would float like a cork.

132
Jupiter's moon Io looks a bit like a pizza. It has many active volcanoes that throw out huge plumes of material, making red blotches and dark marks on its orange-yellow surface.

So far away

133 **Uranus and Neptune are gas giants like Jupiter and Saturn.** They are the next two planets beyond Saturn but much smaller, being less than half as wide. They too have no hard surface. Their cloud tops make Uranus and Neptune both look blue. They are very cold, being so far from the Sun.

▲ There is very little to see on Uranus, just a few wisps of cloud above the greenish haze.

134 **Uranus seems to 'roll' around the Sun.** Unlike most of the other planets, which spin upright like a top, Uranus spins on its side. It may have been knocked over when something crashed into it millions of years ago.

135 **Uranus has more moons than any other planet.** Twenty-one have been discovered so far, although one is so newly discovered it has not got a name yet. Most of them are very small but there are five larger ones.

◄ Miranda is one of Uranus' moons. It looks as though it has been split apart and put back together again.

136

Neptune had a storm that disappeared. When the *Voyager 2* space probe flew past Neptune in 1989 it spotted a huge storm like a dark version of the Great Red Spot on Jupiter. When the Hubble Space Telescope looked at Neptune in 1994, the storm had gone.

137

Neptune has bright blue clouds that make the whole planet look blue. Above these clouds are smaller white streaks. These are icy clouds that race around the planet. One of the white clouds seen by the *Voyager 2* space probe was called 'Scooter' because it scooted around the planet so fast.

138

Neptune is sometimes farther from the Sun than Pluto. All the planets travel around the Sun along orbits (paths) that look like circles, but Pluto's path is more squashed. This sometimes brings it closer to the Sun than Neptune.

▼ In the past, astronomers thought there might be another planet, called Planet X, outside Neptune and Pluto.

Orbit of Neptune

Orbit of Pluto

Orbit of Planet X

◄ Like all the gas giant planets, Neptune has rings. However, they are much darker and thinner than Saturn's rings.

QUIZ

1. How many moons does Uranus have?

2. Which is the biggest planet in our Solar System?

3. Which planet seems to 'roll' around the Sun?

4. What colour are Neptune's clouds?

Answers:
1. 21 2. Jupiter
3. Uranus 4. Blue

139 **There are probably billions of tiny comets at the edge of the Solar System.** They circle the Sun far beyond Pluto. Sometimes one is disturbed and moves inwards towards the Sun, looping around it before going back to where it came from. Some comets come back to the Sun regularly, such as Halley's comet that returns every 76 years.

▶ The solid part of a comet is hidden inside a huge, glowing cloud that stretches into a long tail.

140 **A comet is often called a dirty snowball because it is made of dust and ice mixed together.** Heat from the Sun melts some of the ice. This makes dust and gas stream away from the comet, forming a huge tail that glows in the sunlight.

141 **Comet tails always point away from the Sun.** Although it looks bright, a comet's tail is extremely thin so it is blown outwards, away from the Sun. When the comet moves away from the Sun, its tail goes in front of it.

143 Asteroids are chunks of rock that failed to stick together to make a planet. Most of them circle the Sun between Mars and Jupiter where there would be room for another planet. There are millions of asteroids, some the size of a car, and others as big as mountains.

▶ Asteroids travel in a ring around the Sun. This ring is called the Asteroid belt and can be found between Mars and Jupiter.

142 Meteors are sometimes called shooting stars. They are not really stars, just streaks of light that flash across the night sky. Meteors are made when pebbles racing through space at high speed hit the top of the air above the Earth. The pebble gets so hot it burns up. We see it as a glowing streak for a few seconds.

QUIZ
1. Which way does a comet tail always point?
2. What is another name for a meteor?
3. Where is the asteroid belt?

Answers:
1. Away from the Sun
2. Shooting star
3. Between Mars and Jupiter

▼ At certain times of year there are meteor showers when you can see more shooting stars than usual.

A star is born

144 **Stars are born in clouds of dust and gas in space called nebulae.** Astronomers can see these clouds as shining patches in the night sky, or dark patches against the distant stars. These clouds shrink as gravity pulls the dust and gas together. At the centre, the gas gets hotter and hotter until a new star is born.

▶ Stars are born and die all over the Universe and by looking at stars in different stages of their life, astronomers have learned about the stages of their existence.

1. Clumps of gas in this nebula start to shrink into the tight round balls that will become stars.

2. The gas spirals round as it is pulled inwards. Any left over gas and dust may form planets around the new star.

3. Deep in its centre, the new star starts making energy, but it is still hidden by the cloud of dust and gas.

145 **Stars begin their lives when they start making energy.** When the dust and gas pulls tightly together it gets very hot. Finally it gets so hot in the middle that it can start making energy. The energy makes the star shine, giving out heat and light like the Sun.

4. The dust and gas are blown away and we can see the star shining. Maybe it has a family of planets like the Sun.

146

Young stars often stay together in clusters. When they start to shine they light up the nebula, making it glow with bright colours. Then the starlight blows away the remains of the cloud and we can see a group of new stars, called a star cluster.

▶ This cluster of young stars, with many stars of different colours and sizes, will gradually drift apart, breaking up the cluster.

QUIZ

1. What is a nebula?
2. How long has the Sun been shining?
3. What colour are large hot stars?
4. What is a group of new young stars called?

Answers:
1. A cloud of dust and gas in space 2. About 4 billion years 3. Bluish-white 4. Star cluster

148

Smaller stars live much longer than huge stars. Stars use up their gas to make energy, and the largest stars use up their gas much faster than smaller stars. The Sun is about half way through its life. It has been shining for about 5 billion years and will go on shining for another 5 billion years.

147

Large stars are very hot and white, smaller stars are cooler and redder. A large star can make energy faster and get much hotter than a smaller star. This gives them a very bright, bluish-white colour. Smaller stars are cooler. This makes them look red and shine less brightly. Ordinary in-between stars like our Sun look yellow.

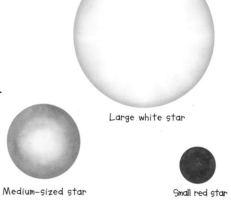

Large white star

Medium-sized star

Small red star

Death of a star

149 **Stars begin to die when they run out of gas to make energy.** The middle of the star begins to shrink but the outer parts expand, making the star much larger.

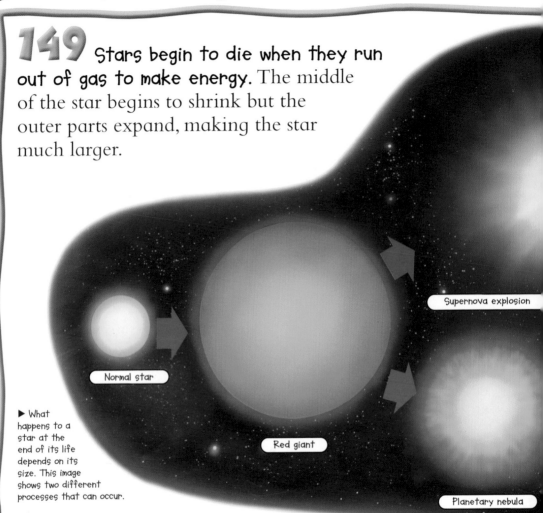

Normal star

Red giant

Supernova explosion

Planetary nebula

▶ What happens to a star at the end of its life depends on its size. This image shows two different processes that can occur.

150 **Red giant stars are dying stars that have swollen to hundreds of times their normal size.** Their expanding outer layers get cooler, making them look red. When the Sun is a red giant it will be large enough to swallow up the nearest planets, Mercury and Venus, and perhaps Earth.

151 **A red giant becomes a white dwarf.** The outer layers drift away, making a halo of gas around the star. The starlight makes this gas glow and we call it a planetary nebula. All that is left is a small, hot star called a white dwarf which cannot make energy and gradually cools and dies.

◀ Giant stars may end in a supernova explosion. This leaves a very tiny, hot neutron star or a black hole.

152 Very heavy stars end their lives in a huge explosion called a supernova.

This explosion blows away all the outer parts of the star. Gas rushes outwards in all directions, making a glowing shell. All that is left is a tiny hot star in the middle of the shell.

Black hole

I DON'T BELIEVE IT!

Astronomers only know that black holes exist because they can see flickers of very hot gas near one just before they are sucked in.

White dwarf

Black dwarf

▲ When a star the same size as our Sun dies, it will swell up into a red giant. Next it will lose its outer layers and shrink down to 100 times smaller, becoming a white dwarf. Finally it will fade to a black dwarf.

153 After a supernova explosion the largest stars may end up as black holes. The remains of the star fall in on itself. As it shrinks, its gravity gets stronger. Eventually the pull of its gravity can get so strong that nothing near it can escape. This is called a black hole.

Billions of galaxies

154 The Sun is part of a huge family of stars called the Milky Way Galaxy. There are billions of other stars in our Galaxy, as many as the grains of sand on a beach. We call it the Milky Way because it looks like a very faint band of light in the night sky, as though someone has spilt some milk across space.

▶ Seen from outside, our Galaxy would look like this. The Sun is towards the edge, in one of the spiral arms.

155 Curling arms give some galaxies their spiral shape. The Milky Way has arms made of bright stars and glowing clouds of gas that curl round into a spiral shape. Some galaxies, called elliptical galaxies, have a round shape like a squashed ball. Other galaxies have no particular shape.

I DON'T BELIEVE IT!

If you could fit the Milky Way onto these two pages, the Sun would be so tiny, you could not see it.

156
There are billions of galaxies outside the Milky Way. Some are larger than the Milky Way and many are smaller, but they all have more stars than you can count. The galaxies tend to stay together in groups called clusters.

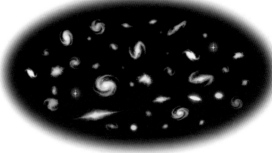

▲ A cluster of galaxies has many different types, with large elliptical and spiral galaxies and many small irregular ones.

▶ These two galaxies are so close that each has pulled a long tail of bright stars from the other.

157
There is no bump when galaxies collide. A galaxy is mostly empty space between the stars. But when galaxies get very close they can pull each other out of shape. Sometimes they look as if they have grown a huge tail stretching out into space, or their shape may change into a ring of glowing stars.

▼ From left to right these are spiral, irregular, and elliptical galaxies, and a spiral galaxy with a bar across the middle.

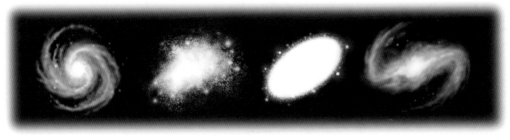

What is the Universe?

158 **The Universe is the name we give to everything we know about.** This means everything on Earth, from tiny bits of dust to the highest mountain, and everything that lives here, including you. It also means everything in space, all the billions of stars in the billions of galaxies.

▼ All the parts that make up the Universe were once packed tightly together. No one knows why the Universe started expanding with a Big Bang.

159 **The Universe started with a massive explosion called the Big Bang.** Astronomers think that this happened about 15 billion years ago. A huge explosion sent everything racing outwards in all directions. To start with, everything was packed incredibly close together. Over time it has expanded (spread out) into the Universe we can see today, which is mostly empty space.

▼ As everything moved apart in all directions, stars and galaxies started to form.

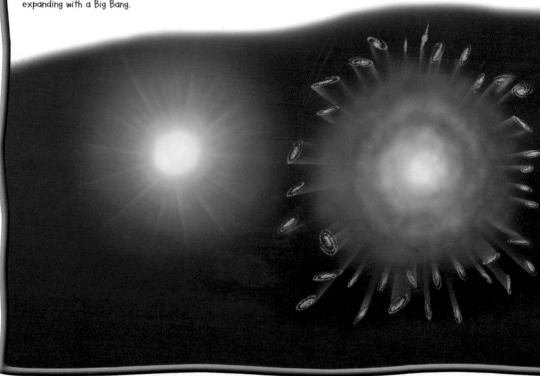

160 The galaxies are still racing away from each other.

When astronomers look at distant galaxies they can see that other galaxies are moving away from our galaxy, and the more distant galaxies are moving away faster. In fact all the galaxies are moving apart from each other. We say that the Universe is expanding.

161 We do not know what will happen to the Universe billions of years in the future.

It may keep on expanding. If this happens old stars will gradually die and no new ones will be born. Everywhere will become dark and cold.

▼ Today there are galaxies of different shapes and sizes, all moving apart. One day they may start moving towards each other.

162 The Universe may end with a Big Crunch.

This means that the galaxies would all start coming closer together. In the end the galaxies and stars would all be crushed together in a Big Crunch, the opposite of the Big Bang explosion.

DOTTY UNIVERSE

You will need:
a balloon

Blow up a balloon a little, holding the neck to stop air escaping. Mark dots on the balloon with a pen, then blow it up some more. Watch how the dots move apart from each other. This is like the galaxies moving apart as the Universe expands.

▼ The Universe could end as it began, all packed incredibly close together.

75

Looking into space

163 People have imagined they can see the outlines of people and animals in the star patterns in the sky.

These patterns are called constellations. Hundreds of years ago astronomers named the constellations to help them find their way around the skies.

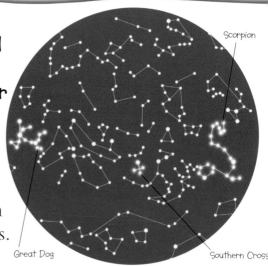

▲ If you live south of the Equator, these are the constellations you can see at night.

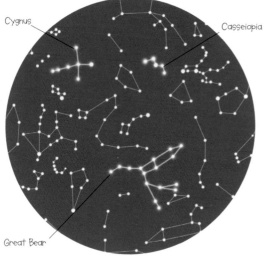

▲ From the north of the Equator, you can see a different set of constellations in the night sky.

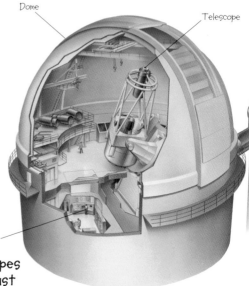

▲ A huge dome protects this large telescope. It opens to let the telescope point at the sky, and both the dome and telescope can turn to look at any part of the sky.

164 Astronomers use huge telescopes to see much more than we can see with just our eyes. Telescopes make things look bigger and nearer. They also show faint, glowing clouds of gas, and distant stars and galaxies.

▲ The Hubble Space Telescope takes much more detailed pictures and can see farther than any similar telescope.

165 Space telescopes look even further to find exciting things in deep space. On Earth, clouds often hide the stars and the air is always moving, which blurs the pictures made by the telescopes. A telescope in space above the air can make clearer pictures. The Hubble Space Telescope has been circling the Earth for more than 10 years sending back beautiful pictures.

166 Astronomers also look at radio signals from space. They use telescopes that look like huge satellite TV dishes. These make pictures using the radio signals that come from space. The pictures do not always look like those from ordinary telescopes, but they can spot exciting things that most ordinary telescopes cannot see, such as jets of gas from black holes.

MOON-WATCH
You will need:
binoculars

On a clear night look at the Moon through binoculars, holding them very steady. You will be able to see the round shapes of craters. Binoculars are really two telescopes, one for each eye, and they make the Moon look bigger so you can see more detail.

▼ Radio telescopes often have rows of dishes like these to collect radio signals from space. Altogether, they act like one much larger dish to make more detailed pictures. The dishes can move to look in any direction.

Three, two, one... Lift-off!

167 To blast into space, a rocket has to travel nearly 40 times faster than a jumbo jet. If it goes any slower, gravity pulls it back to Earth. Rockets are powered by burning fuel, which makes hot gases. These gases rush out of the engines, shooting the rocket forwards.

Satellite goes into space

▶ Each stage fires its engine to make the rocket go faster and faster until it puts the satellite into space.

Third stage

First stage

Second stage

Booster rockets drop away

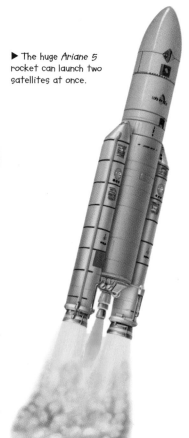

▶ The huge *Ariane 5* rocket can launch two satellites at once.

168 A single rocket is not powerful enough to launch a satellite or spacecraft into space. So rockets have two or three stages, which are really separate rockets mounted on top of each other, each with its own engines. When the first stage has used up its fuel it drops away, and the second stage starts. Finally the third stage takes over to go into space.

169

The space shuttle takes off from Earth as a rocket. It has rocket engines that burn fuel from a huge tank. But it also needs two large booster rockets to give it extra speed. The boosters drop away after two minutes, and the main rocket tank after six.

ROCKET POWER

You will need:
a balloon

If you blow up a balloon and let it go, the balloon shoots off across the room. The air inside the balloon has rushed out, pushing the balloon away in the opposite direction. A rocket blasting into space works in a similar way.

170

The shuttle lands back on Earth on a long runway, just like a giant glider. It does not use any engines for the landing, unlike an aircraft. It touches down so fast, the pilot uses a parachute as well as brakes to stop it on the runway.

▼ The shuttle puts down its wheels and lands on the runway.

▲ The shuttle is blasted into space by three rocket engines and two huge booster rockets.

Living in space

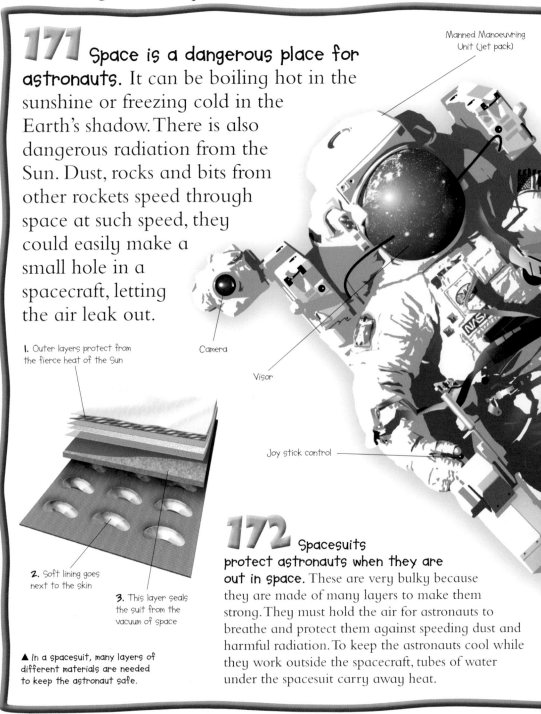

171 **Space is a dangerous place for astronauts.** It can be boiling hot in the sunshine or freezing cold in the Earth's shadow. There is also dangerous radiation from the Sun. Dust, rocks and bits from other rockets speed through space at such speed, they could easily make a small hole in a spacecraft, letting the air leak out.

Manned Manoeuvring Unit (jet pack)

Camera

Visor

Joy stick control

1. Outer layers protect from the fierce heat of the Sun

2. Soft lining goes next to the skin

3. This layer seals the suit from the vacuum of space

▲ In a spacesuit, many layers of different materials are needed to keep the astronaut safe.

172 **Spacesuits protect astronauts when they are out in space.** These are very bulky because they are made of many layers to make them strong. They must hold the air for astronauts to breathe and protect them against speeding dust and harmful radiation. To keep the astronauts cool while they work outside the spacecraft, tubes of water under the spacesuit carry away heat.

SPACE MEALS

You will need:

dried noodles   boiling water

Buy a dried snack such as noodles, that just needs boiling water added. This is the kind of food astronauts eat. Most of their meals are dried so they are not too heavy to launch into space.

Glove

Spacesuit

173 Everything floats around in space as if it has no weight. So all objects have to be fixed down or they will float away. Astronauts have footholds to keep them still while they are working. They strap themselves into sleeping bags so they don't bump into things when they are asleep.

▲ Sleeping bags are fixed to a wall so astronauts look as though they are asleep standing up.

174 Astronauts must take everything they need into space with them. Out in space there is no air, water or food so all the things that astronauts need to live must be packed into their spacecraft and taken with them.

Home from home

175 A space station is a home in space for astronauts and cosmonauts (Russian astronauts). It has a kitchen for making meals, and cabins with sleeping bags. There are toilets, wash basins and sometimes showers. They have places to work and controls where astronauts can check that everything is working properly.

176 The International Space Station, ISS, is being built in space. This is the latest and largest space station. Sixteen countries are helping to build it including the US, Russia, Japan, Canada, Brazil and 11 European countries. It is built up from separate sections called modules that have been made to fit together like a jigsaw.

I DON'T BELIEVE IT!

The US space station *Skylab*, launched in 1973, fell back to Earth in 1979. Most of it landed in the ocean but some pieces hit Australia.

KEY
1. Solar panels for power
2. Docking port
3. Space shuttle
4. Control module
5. Living module
6. Soyuz ferry

177 Each part is launched from Earth and added to the ISS in space. There they are fitted by astronauts at the ISS using the shuttle's robot arm. Huge panels of solar cells are added. These turn sunlight into electricity to give a power supply for the space station.

◄ When all the pieces have been put into place, the International Space Station will look like this as it circles the Earth.

178 The crew live on board the ISS for several months at a time. The first crew of three people arrived at the space station in November 2000 and stayed for over four months. When the space station is finished there will be room for seven astronauts and they will have six modules where they can live and work.

179 The US shuttle carries astronauts, supplies and equipment up to the ISS. It docks for about a week before returning to Earth. Russia has a *Soyuz* spacecraft for ferrying people to and from the space station and a *Progress* ship which brings fresh supplies.

Robot explorers

180 **Robot spacecraft called probes have explored all the planets.** Probes travel in space to take close-up pictures and measurements. They send the information back to scientists on Earth. Some probes circle planets taking pictures. For a really close-up look, a probe can land on the surface.

Power supply

Radio dish sends messages to Earth

Cameras

▲ Voyager 2 gave us close-up pictures of four different planets.

181 **In 1976, two *Viking* spacecraft landed on Mars to look for life.** They scooped up some dust and tested it to see if any tiny creatures lived on Mars. They did not find any signs of life and their pictures showed only a dry, red, dusty desert.

182 **Two *Voyager* probes left Earth in 1977 to visit the gas giant planets.** They reached Jupiter in 1979, flying past and on to Saturn. *Voyager 2* went on to visit Uranus and then Neptune in 1989. It sent back thousands of pictures of each planet as it flew past.

▼ The *Viking* landers took soil samples from Mars, but found no sign of life.

▲ When *Galileo* has finished sending back pictures of Jupiter and its moons, it will plunge into Jupiter's swirling clouds.

183

Galileo has circled Jupiter for more than six years. It arrived in 1995 and dropped a small probe into Jupiter's clouds. Galileo sent back pictures of the planet and its largest moons. It was discovered that two of them may have water hidden under ice thicker than the Arctic ice on Earth.

▼ *Sojourner* spent three months on Mars. The small rover was about the size of a microwave oven.

QUIZ

1. When did the *Voyager* probes fly past Jupiter?

2. Which probe sent pictures of Jupiter's clouds?

3. Which probes tested the dust on Mars for signs of life?

4. What was the name of the *Mars Pathfinder* rover?

Answers:
1. 1979 2. *Galileo*
3. *Viking* 4. *Sojourner*

184

Mars Pathfinder carried a small rover called *Sojourner* to Mars in 1997. It landed on the surface and opened up to let *Sojourner* out. This rover was like a remote control car, but with six wheels. It tested the soil and rocks to find out what they were made of as it slowly drove around the landing site.

Watching the Earth

185 **Hundreds of satellites circle the Earth in space.** They are launched into space by rockets and may stay there for ten years or more.

▶ Weather satellites look down at the clouds and give warning when a violent storm is approaching.

186 **Communications satellites carry TV programmes and telephone messages around the world.** Large aerials on Earth beam radio signals up to a space satellite which then beams them down to another aerial, half way round the world. This lets us talk to people on the other side of the world, and watch events such as the Olympics Games while they are happening in faraway countries.

▼ Communications satellites can beam TV programmes directly to your home through your own aerial dish.

187 **Weather satellites help the forecasters tell us what the weather will be like.** These satellites can see where the clouds are forming and which way they are going. They watch the winds and rain and measure how hot the air and the ground are.

▶ The different satellites each have their own job to do, looking at the Earth, or the weather, or out into space.

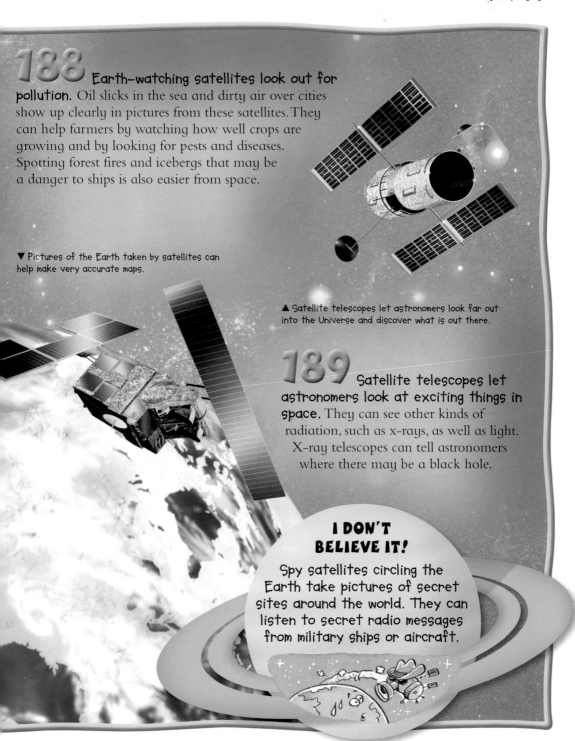

188 **Earth-watching satellites look out for pollution.** Oil slicks in the sea and dirty air over cities show up clearly in pictures from these satellites. They can help farmers by watching how well crops are growing and by looking for pests and diseases. Spotting forest fires and icebergs that may be a danger to ships is also easier from space.

▼ Pictures of the Earth taken by satellites can help make very accurate maps.

▲ Satellite telescopes let astronomers look far out into the Universe and discover what is out there.

189 **Satellite telescopes let astronomers look at exciting things in space.** They can see other kinds of radiation, such as x-rays, as well as light. X-ray telescopes can tell astronomers where there may be a black hole.

I DON'T BELIEVE IT!

Spy satellites circling the Earth take pictures of secret sites around the world. They can listen to secret radio messages from military ships or aircraft.

Voyage to the Moon

190 **The first men landed on the Moon in 1969.** They were three astronauts from the US *Apollo 11* mission. Neil Armstrong was the first person to set foot on the Moon. Only five other *Apollo* missions have landed on the Moon since then.

191 **A giant *Saturn 5* rocket launched the astronauts on their journey to the Moon.** It was the largest rocket that had ever been built. Its three huge stages lifted the astronauts into space, and then the third stage gave the spacecraft an extra boost to send it to the Moon.

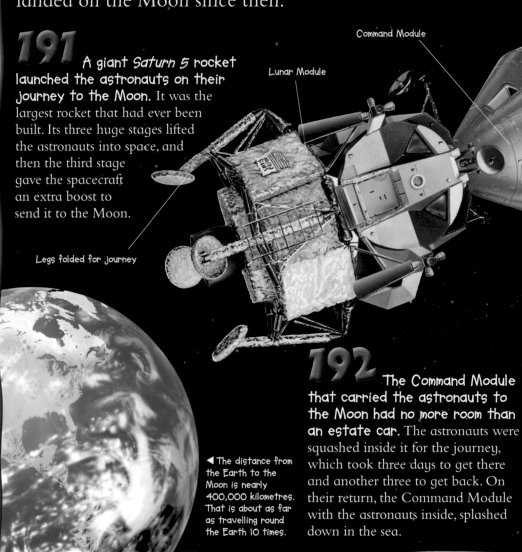

Command Module

Lunar Module

Legs folded for journey

◀ The distance from the Earth to the Moon is nearly 400,000 kilometres. That is about as far as travelling round the Earth 10 times.

192 **The Command Module that carried the astronauts to the Moon had no more room than an estate car.** The astronauts were squashed inside it for the journey, which took three days to get there and another three to get back. On their return, the Command Module with the astronauts inside, splashed down in the sea.

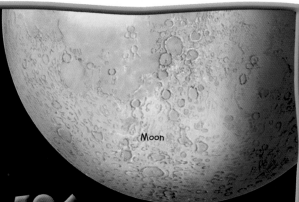

Thrusters

Main engine

Service Module with
fuel and air supplies

Moon

▲ The Lunar and Command Modules travelled to the Moon fixed together, then separated for the Moon landing.

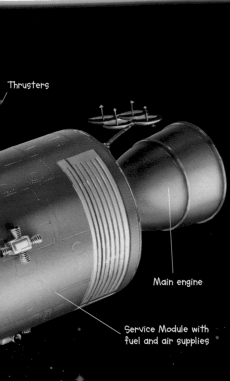

194 The Lunar Rover was a moon car for the astronauts to ride on. It looked like a buggy with four wheels and two seats. It could only travel about as fast as you can run.

195 No one has been back to the Moon since the last *Apollo* mission left in 1972. Astronauts had visited six different places on the Moon and brought back enough Moon rock to keep scientists busy for many years. Maybe one day people will return to the Moon and build bases where they can live and work.

193 The Lunar Module took two of the astronauts to the Moon's surface. Once safely landed they put on spacesuits and went outside to collect rocks. Later they took off in the Lunar Module to join the third astronaut who had stayed in the Command Module, circling above the Moon on his own.

I DON'T BELIEVE IT!

On the way to the Moon an explosion damaged the *Apollo 13* spacecraft, leaving the astronauts with little heat or light.

Are we alone?

196 The only life we have found so far in the Universe is here on Earth. Everywhere you look on Earth from the frozen Antarctic to the hottest, driest deserts, on land and in the sea, there are living things. Some are huge, such as whales and elephants and others are much too small to see. But they all need water to live.

▲ On Earth, animals can live in many different habitats, such as in the sea, the air, in deserts and jungles, and icy lands. How many different habitats can you see here?

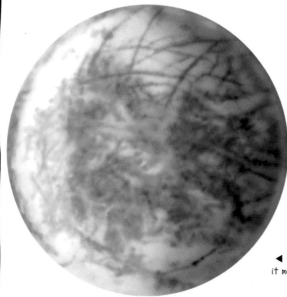

197 There may be an underground ocean on Europa, one of Jupiter's moons. Europa is a little smaller than our Moon and is covered in ice. However, astronomers think that there may be an ocean of water under the ice. If so, there could be strange living creatures swimming around deep underground.

◄ Deep beneath the cracked, icy surface of Europa, it may be warm enough for the ice to melt into water.

198 Astronomers have found signs of planets circling other stars, but none like the Earth so far. The planets they have found are large ones like Jupiter, but they keep looking for a planet with a solid surface which is not too hot or too cold. They are looking for one where there might be water and living things.

◄ No-one knows what other planets would be like. They could have strange moons or colourful rings. Anything that lives there might look very strange to us.

199 Mars seems to have had rivers and seas billions of years ago. Astronomers can see dry river beds and ridges that look like ocean shores on Mars. This makes them think Mars may have been warm and wet long ago and something may have lived there. Now it is very cold and dry with no sign of life.

I DON'T BELIEVE IT!
It would take thousands of years to get to the nearest stars with our present spacecraft.

▼ This message could tell people living on distant planets about the Earth, and the people who live here.

200 Scientists have sent a radio message to a distant group of stars. They are hoping that anyone living there will understand the message about life on Earth. However, it will take 25,000 years to get to the stars and another 25,000 years for a reply to come back to Earth!

Outside, inside

201 **There are more than six billion human beings in the world.** If you could say hello to all of them, even quickly, it would take you more than 300 years. In some ways, all human bodies are very similar, especially on the inside. Each one has a heart and brain, bones and guts, arms and legs and skin. But each human body is also individual, especially on the outside. You have your own appearance, size and shape, facial features, hairstyle and clothes. You also have your own personality, with likes and dislikes, and special things that make you happy or sad. So human bodies may be very similar in how they look, but not in what they do. You are unique, your own self.

▶ We tend to notice small differences on the outside of human bodies, such as height, width, hair colour and clothes. This allows us to recognize our family and friends.

Baby body

Successful sperm

Egg cell

202 A full-grown human body is made of billions of microscopic parts, called cells. But in the beginning, the body is a single cell, smaller than this full stop. Yet it contains all the instructions, known as genes, for the whole body to grow and develop.

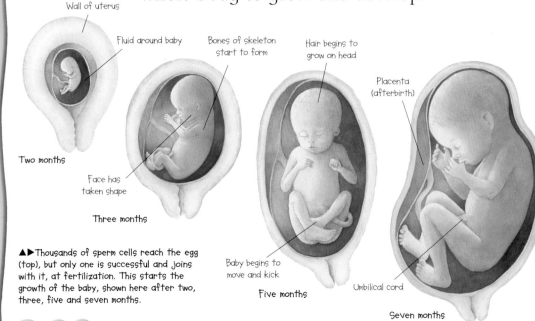

Wall of uterus

Fluid around baby

Bones of skeleton start to form

Hair begins to grow on head

Placenta (afterbirth)

Two months

Face has taken shape

Three months

Baby begins to move and kick

Five months

Umbilical cord

Seven months

▲▶Thousands of sperm cells reach the egg (top), but only one is successful and joins with it, at fertilization. This starts the growth of the baby, shown here after two, three, five and seven months.

203 The body begins when an egg cell inside the mother joins up with sperm from the father. The egg cell splits into two cells, then into four cells, then eight, and so on. The bundle of cells embeds itself in the mother's womb (uterus), which protects and nourishes it. Soon there are thousands of cells, then millions, forming a tiny embryo. After two months the embryo has grown into a tiny baby, as big as your thumb, with arms, legs, eyes, ears and mouth.

204 After nine months in the womb, the baby is ready to be born. Strong muscles in the walls of the womb tighten, or contract. They push the baby through the opening, or neck of the womb, called the cervix, and along the birth canal. The baby enters the outside world.

205 A newborn baby may be frightened and usually starts to cry. Inside the womb it was warm, wet, dark, quiet and cramped. Outside there are lights, noises, voices, fresh air and room to stretch. The crying is also helpful to start the baby breathing, using its own lungs.

I DON'T BELIEVE IT!

The human body never grows as fast again as it does during the first weeks in the womb. If the body kept growing at that rate, every day for 50 years, it would be bigger than the biggest mountain in the world!

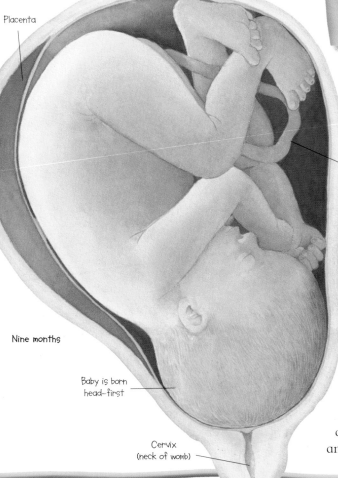

Wall of womb is stretched

Placenta

Nine months

Baby is born head-first

Cervix (neck of womb)

◀ Inside the womb, the baby cannot breathe air or eat food. Nutrients and oxygen pass from mother to baby through the blood vessels in the ropelike umbilical cord.

Umbilical cord

206 Being born can take an hour or two – or a whole day or two. It is very tiring for both the baby and its mother. After birth, the baby starts to feel hungry and it feeds on its mother's milk. Finally, mother and baby settle down for a rest and some sleep.

The growing body

207 **A new baby just seems to eat, sleep and cry.** It feeds on milk when hungry and sleeps when tired. Also, it cries when it is too hot, too cold, or when its nappy needs changing.

208 **A new baby is not totally helpless.** It can do simple actions called reflexes, to help it survive. If something touches the baby's cheek, it turns its head to that side and tries to suck. If the baby hears a loud noise, it opens its eyes wide, throws out its arms and cries for help. If something touches the baby's hand and fingers, it grasps tightly.

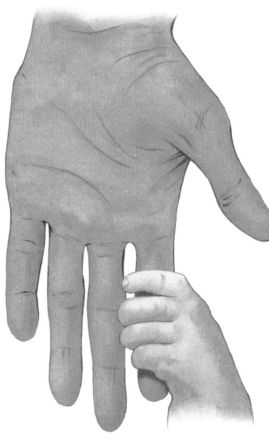

▲ In the grasping reflex, the baby tightly holds anything that touches its hand or fingers. Its grip is surprisingly strong!

WHAT HAPPENS WHEN?

Most babies learn to do certain actions in the same order. The order is mixed up here. Can you put it right?

walk, crawl, roll over, sit up, smile, stand

Answers:
smile, roll over, sit up, crawl, stand, walk

209 **A new baby looks, listens, touches and quickly learns.** Gradually it starts to recognize voices, faces and places. After about six weeks, it begins to smile. Inside the body, the baby's brain is learning very quickly. The baby soon knows that if it laughs, people will laugh back. If it cries, someone will come to look after it.

▼ Most babies crawl before they walk, but some go straight from sitting or 'bottom-shuffling' to walking.

211 As a baby grows into a child, at around 18 months, it learns ten new words every day, from 'cat' and 'dog' to 'sun' and 'moon'. There are new games such as piling up bricks, new actions such as throwing and kicking, and new skills such as using a spoon at mealtimes and scribbling on paper.

210 At about three months old, most babies can reach out to hold something, and roll over when lying down. By the age of six months, most babies can sit up and hold food in their fingers. At nine months, many babies are crawling well and perhaps standing up. By their first birthday, many babies are learning to walk and starting to talk.

212 At the age of five, when most children start school, they continue to learn an amazing amount. This includes thinking or mental skills such as counting and reading, and precise movements such as writing and drawing. They learn out of the classroom too – how to play with friends and share.

▶ Playing is lots of fun, but it's learning too, as children develop control over the muscles in their fast-growing bodies.

On the body's outside

213 Skin's surface is made of tiny cells which have filled up with a hard, tough substance called keratin, and then died. So when you look at a human body, most of what you see is 'dead'! The cells get rubbed off as you move, have a wash and get dry.

214 Skin rubs off all the time, and grows all the time too. Just under the surface, living cells make more new cells that gradually fill with keratin, die and move up to the surface. It takes about four weeks from a new skin cell being made to when it reaches the surface and is rubbed off. This upper layer of skin is called the epidermis.

▲ Skin may feel smooth, but its surface is made of millions of tiny flakes, far too small to see.

▼ This view shows skin magnified (enlarged) about 50 times.

215 Skin's lower layer, the dermis, is thicker than the epidermis. It is made of tiny, bendy, threadlike fibres of the substance collagen. The dermis also contains small blood vessels, tiny sweat glands, and micro-sensors that detect touch.

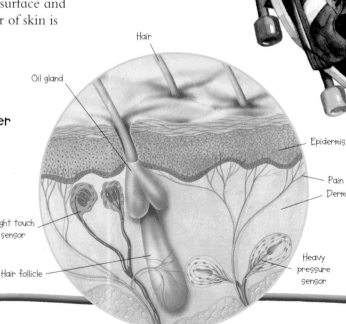

Hair

Oil gland

Light touch sensor

Hair follicle

Epidermis

Pain

Derm

Heavy pressure sensor

▼ Skin is tough, but it sometimes needs help to protect the body. Otherwise it, and the body parts beneath, may get damaged.

Safety helmet protects head and brain

Elbow-pads cushion fall

Knee-pads prevent hard bumps

Gloves save fingers from scrapes and breaks

217 **Skin helps to keep the body at the same temperature.** If you become too hot, sweat oozes onto your skin and, as it dries, draws heat from the body. Also, the blood vessels in the lower layer of skin widen, to lose more heat through the skin. This is why a hot person looks sweaty and red in the face.

218 **Skin gives us our sense of touch.** Millions of microscopic sensors in the lower layer of skin, the dermis, are joined by nerves to the brain. Different sensors detect different kinds of touch, from a light stroke to heavy pressure, heat or cold, and movement. Pain sensors detect when skin is damaged. Ouch!

SENSITIVE SKIN

You will need:

a friend   sticky-tack
two used matchsticks   ruler

1. Press some sticky-tack on the end of the ruler. Press two matchsticks into the sticky-tack, standing upright, about 1 centimetre apart.
2. Make your friend look away. Touch the back of their hand with both matchstick ends. Ask your friend: 'Is that one matchstick or two?' Sensitive skin can detect both ends
3. Try this at several places, such as on the finger, wrist, forearm, neck and cheek.

216 **One of skin's important jobs is to protect the body.** It stops the delicate inner parts from being rubbed, knocked or scraped. Skin also prevents body fluids from leaking away and it keeps out dirt and germs.

Hair and nails

219 **There are about 120,000 hairs on the head, called scalp hairs.** There are also eyebrow hairs and eyelash hairs. Grown-ups have hairs in the armpits and between the legs, and men have hairs on the face. And everyone, even a baby, has tiny hairs all over the body – 20 million of them!

Black curly hair is the result of black melanin from a flat hair follicle

Blonde wavy hair is the result of carotene from an oval hair follicle

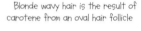

◀ Hair contains pigments (coloured substances) – mainly melanin (dark brown) and some carotene (yellowish). Different amounts of pigments, and the way their tiny particles are spread out, cause different hair colours.

Straight red hair is the result of red melanin from a round hair follicle

Straight black hair is the result of black melanin from a round follicle

220 **Each hair grows from a deep pit in the skin, called a follicle.** The hair is only alive where it gets longer, at its base or root, in the bottom of the follicle. The rest of the hair, called the shaft, is like the surface of the skin – hard, tough, dead and made of keratin. Hair helps to protect the body, especially where it is thicker and longer on the head. It also helps to keep the body warm in cold conditions.

221 **Scalp hairs get longer by about 3 millimetres each week, on average.** Eyebrow hairs grow more slowly. No hairs live for ever. Each one grows for a time, then it falls out, and its follicle has a 'rest' before a new hair sprouts. This is happening all the time, so the body always has some hairs on each part.

222
Nails, like hairs, grow at their base (the nail root) and are made of keratin. Also like hairs, nails grow faster in summer than in winter, and faster at night than by day. Nails lengthen by about half a millimetre, on average, each week.

▼ The growing nail root is hidden under skin. The nail slides slowly along the nail bed.

Nail root

Cuticle (skin edge)

Nail bed

Bone inside finger

▶ Nails make the fingertips stronger and more rigid for pressing hard on guitar strings. Slightly longer nails pluck the strings.

223
Nails have many uses, from peeling off sticky labels to plucking guitar strings or scratching an itch. They protect and stiffen the ends of the fingers, where there are nerves that give us our sense of touch.

I DON'T BELIEVE IT!

A scalp hair grows for up to five years before it falls out and gets replaced. Left uncut during this time, it would be about one metre long. But some people have unusual hair that grows faster and for longer. Each hair can reach more than 5 metres in length before dropping out.

The bony body

224 The human body is strengthened, supported and held up by parts that we cannot see – bones. Without bones, the body would be as floppy as a jellyfish! Bones do many jobs. The long bones in the arms work like levers to reach out the hands. The finger bones grasp and grip. The leg bones are also levers when we walk and run. Bones protect softer body parts. The domelike skull protects the brain. The ribs in the chest are like the bars of a cage to protect the heart and lungs inside. Bones also produce blood cells, as explained on the opposite page.

▶ The skeleton forms a strong framework inside the body. The only artificial (man-made) substances that can match bone for strength and lightness are some of the materials used to make racing cars and jet planes.

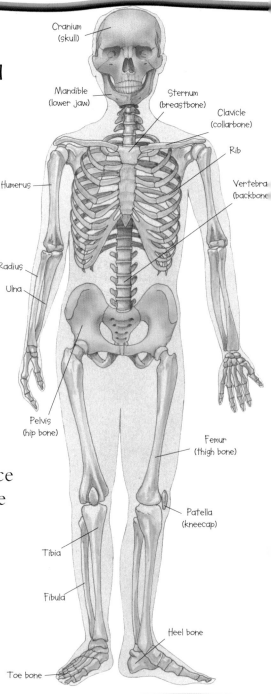

Cranium
(skull)

Mandible
(lower jaw)

Sternum
(breastbone)

Clavicle
(collarbone)

Rib

Humerus

Vertebra
(backbone

Radius

Ulna

Pelvis
(hip bone)

Femur
(thigh bone)

Patella
(kneecap)

Tibia

Fibula

Heel bone

Toe bone

225
All the bones together make up the skeleton. Most people have 206 bones, from head to toe as follows:

- 8 in the upper part of the skull, the cranium or braincase
- 14 in the face
- 6 tiny ear bones, 3 deep in each ear
- 1 in the neck, which is floating and not directly connected to any other bone
- 26 in the spinal column or backbone
- 25 in the chest, being 24 ribs and the breastbone
- 32 in each arm, from shoulder to fingertips (8 in each wrist)
- 31 in each leg, from hip to toetips (7 in each ankle)

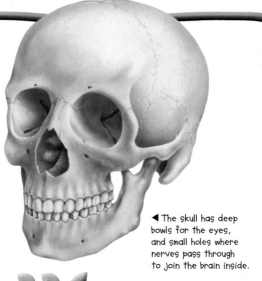

◄ The skull has deep bowls for the eyes, and small holes where nerves pass through to join the brain inside.

NAME THE BONE!
Every bone has a scientific or medical name, and many have ordinary names too. Can you match up these ordinary and scientific names for various bones?

1. Mandible 2. Femur 3. Clavicle
4. Pelvis 5. Patella 6. Sternum

a. Thigh bone b. Breastbone
c. Kneecap d. Hip bone
e. Collarbone f. Lower jaw bone

Answers:
1f 2a 3e 4d 5c 6b

226
Bone contains threads of the tough, slightly bendy substance called collagen. It also has hard minerals such as calcium and phosphate. Together, the collagen and minerals make a bone strong and rigid, yet able to bend slightly under stress. Bones have blood vessels for nourishment and nerves to feel pressure and pain. Also, some bones are not solid. They contain a jellylike substance called marrow. This makes tiny parts for the blood, called red and white blood cells.

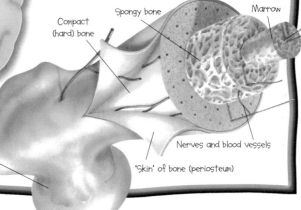

Spongy bone

Marrow

Compact (hard) bone

Nerves and blood vessels

'Skin' of bone (periosteum)

End or head of bone

▶ Bone has a hard layer outside, a spongy layer next, and soft marrow in the middle.

The flexible body

227 Without joints, almost the only parts of your body that could move would be your tongue and eyebrows! Joints between bones allow the skeleton to bend. You have more than 150 joints. The largest are in the hips and knees. The smallest are in the fingers, toes, and between the tiny bones inside each ear which help you hear.

228 There are several kinds of joints, depending on the shapes of the bone ends, and how much the bones can move. Bend your knee and your lower leg moves forwards and backwards, but not sideways. This is a hinge-type joint. Bend your hip and your leg can move forwards, backwards, and also from side to side. This is a ball-and-socket joint.

▶ In the shoulder, the upper arm bone's rounded head fits into a socket in the shoulder blade.

Collarbone

Head of upper arm bone

Shoulder blade

TEST YOUR JOINTS
Try using these different joints carefully, and see how much movement they allow. Can you guess the type of joint used in each one – hinge or ball-and-socket?

1. Fingertip joint (smallest knuckle)
2. Elbow
3. Hip
4. Shoulder

229 Inside a joint where the bones come together, each bone end is covered with a smooth, shiny, slippery, slightly springy substance, known as cartilage. This is smeared with a thick liquid called synovial fluid. The fluid works like the oil in a car, to smooth the movements and reduce rubbing and wear between the cartilage surfaces.

Answers:
1. hinge 2. hinge
3. ball-and-socket 4. ball-and-socket

230

The bones in a joint are linked together by a baglike part, the capsule, and strong, stretchy, straplike ligaments. The ligaments let the bones move but stop them coming apart or moving too far. The shoulder has seven strong ligaments.

◀ The arm joints are very flexible, but they can also work as strongly as the leg joints to hold up the whole body.

231

In some joints, there are cartilage coverings over the bone ends and also pads of cartilage between the cartilage! These extra pads are called articular discs. There is one in each joint in the backbone, between the spinal bones, which are called vertebrae. There are also two of these extra cartilages, known as menisci, in each knee joint. They help the knee to 'lock' straight so that we can stand up without too much effort.

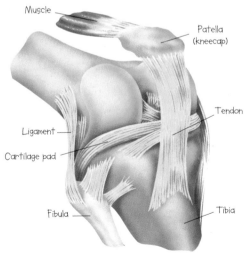

Muscle

Patella
(kneecap)

Tendon

Ligament

Cartilage pad

Fibula

Tibia

▲ The knee has many ligaments, cartilage pads (menisci) and strong tendons that anchor muscles.

105

When muscles pull

232 Almost half the body's weight is muscles, and there are more than 640 of them! Muscles have one simple but important job, which is to get shorter, or contract. A muscle cannot get longer.

233 A muscle is joined to a bone by its tendon. This is where the end of the muscle becomes slimmer or tapers, and is strengthened by strong, thick fibres of collagen. The fibres are fixed firmly into the surface of the bone.

▼ A tendon is stuck firmly into the bone it pulls, with a joint stronger than superglue!

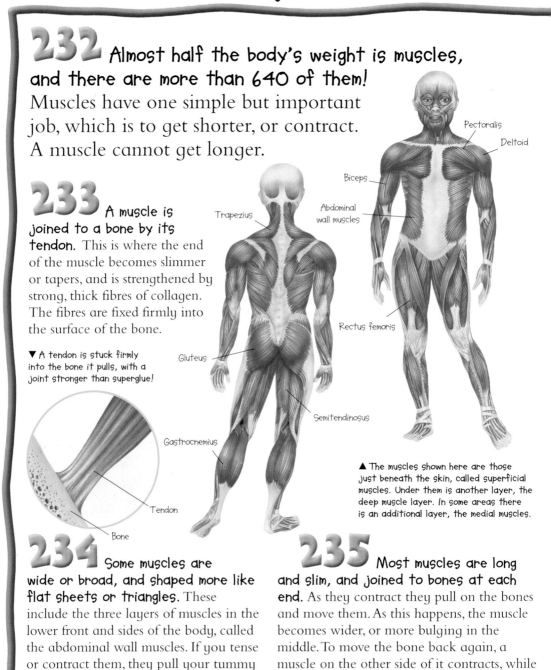

Pectoralis

Deltoid

Biceps

Trapezius

Abdominal wall muscles

Rectus femoris

Gluteus

Semitendinosus

Gastrocnemius

Tendon

Bone

▲ The muscles shown here are those just beneath the skin, called superficial muscles. Under them is another layer, the deep muscle layer. In some areas there is an additional layer, the medial muscles.

234 Some muscles are wide or broad, and shaped more like flat sheets or triangles. These include the three layers of muscles in the lower front and sides of the body, called the abdominal wall muscles. If you tense or contract them, they pull your tummy in to make you look thinner.

235 Most muscles are long and slim, and joined to bones at each end. As they contract they pull on the bones and move them. As this happens, the muscle becomes wider, or more bulging in the middle. To move the bone back again, a muscle on the other side of it contracts, while the first muscle relaxes and is pulled longer.

◀ A weightlifter's muscles can raise more than three times the body weight above the head.

I DON'T BELIEVE IT!

It's easier to smile than to frown. There are about 40 muscles under the skin of the face. You use almost all of these to make a deep frown, but only about half of them to show a broad grin.

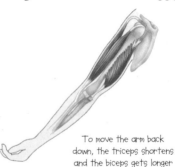

236 Every muscle in the body has a scientific or medical name, which is often quite long and complicated. Some of these names are familiar to people who do exercise and sports. The 'pecs' are the pectoralis major muscles across the chest. The 'biceps' are the biceps brachii muscles in the upper arms, which bulge when you bend your elbow.

237 If you take plenty of exercise or play sport, you do not gain new muscles. But the muscles you have become larger and stronger. This keeps them fit and healthy. Muscles which are not used much may become weak and floppy.

▶ Muscles work in two-way pairs, like the biceps and triceps, which bend and straighten the elbow.

Biceps

Triceps

Biceps gets shorter and the elbow moves

To move the arm back down, the triceps shortens and the biceps gets longer

Muscle power

238 **Muscles have many shapes and sizes, but inside they are all similar.** They have bundles of long, hairlike threads called muscle fibres, or myofibres. Each muscle fibre is slightly thinner than a hair. A big muscle has many thousands of them. Most are about 3 or 4 centimetres long. In a big muscle, many fibres of different lengths lie alongside each other and end-to-end.

Muscle fibre

Nerve branches

Muscle fibre

Muscle fibril

▶ While arm muscles prepare to make the racket hit the ball, hundreds of other muscles keep the body poised and balanced.

239 **Each muscle fibre is made of dozens or hundreds of even thinner parts, called muscle fibrils or myofibrils.** There are millions of these in a large muscle. And, as you may guess, each fibril contains hundreds of yet thinner threads! There are two kinds, actin and myosin. As the actins slide past and between the myosins, the threads get shorter – and the muscle contracts.

240

Muscles are controlled by the brain, which sends messages to them along stringlike nerves. When a muscle contracts for a long time, its fibres 'take turns'. Some of them shorten powerfully while others relax, then the contracted ones relax while others shorten, and so on.

Body of muscle

◀ The main part of a muscle is the body or belly, with hundreds of muscle fibres inside.

▼ Dozens of arm and hand muscles move a pen precisely, a tiny amount each time.

Actin

Myosin

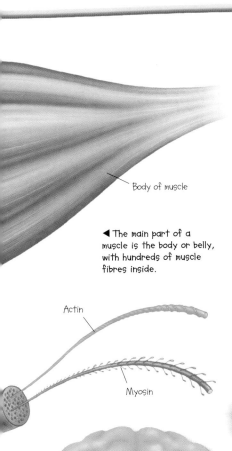

WHICH MUSCLES?

Can you match the names of these muscles with different parts of the body?

a. Gluteus maximus b. Masseter
c. Sartorius d. Cardiac muscle
e. Pectoralis major

1. Heart 2. Chest 3. Front of thigh
4. Buttock 5. Mouth

Answers:
a4 b5 c3 d1 e2

241

The body's biggest muscles are the ones you sit on – the gluteus maximus muscles in the buttocks. The longest muscle is the sartorius, across the front of the thigh. Some of its fibres are more than 30 centimetres in length. The most powerful muscle, for its size, is the masseter in the lower cheek, which closes the jaws when you chew.

The breathing body

242 **The body cannot survive more than a minute or two without breathing.** This action is so important, we do it all the time without thinking. We breathe to take air into the body. Air contains the gas oxygen, which is needed to get energy from food to power all of the body's vital life processes.

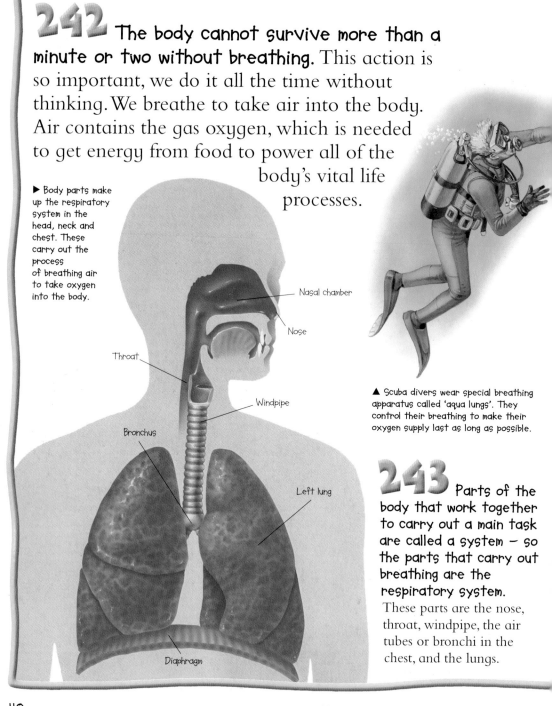

► Body parts make up the respiratory system in the head, neck and chest. These carry out the process of breathing air to take oxygen into the body.

Nasal chamber

Nose

Throat

Windpipe

Bronchus

Left lung

Diaphragm

▲ Scuba divers wear special breathing apparatus called 'aqua lungs'. They control their breathing to make their oxygen supply last as long as possible.

243 **Parts of the body that work together to carry out a main task are called a system – so the parts that carry out breathing are the respiratory system.** These parts are the nose, throat, windpipe, the air tubes or bronchi in the chest, and the lungs.

◀ The human voice can make a wide range of sounds, from loud to soft, and low to high.

244 The nose is the entrance for fresh air to the lungs — and the exit for stale air from the lungs. The soft, moist lining inside the nose makes air warmer and damper, which is better for the lungs. Tiny bits of floating dust and germs stick to the lining or the hairs in the nose, making the air cleaner.

245 The windpipe, or trachea, is a tube leading from the back of the nose and mouth, down to the lungs. It has about 20 C-shaped hoops of cartilage in its wall to keep it open, like a vacuum cleaner hose. Otherwise the pressure of body parts in the neck and chest would squash it shut.

HUMMMMMM!

You will need:

stopwatch

Do you think making sounds with your voice-box uses more air than breathing? Find out by following this experiment.

1. Take a deep breath in, then breathe out at your normal rate, for as long as you can. Time the out-breath.

2. Take a similar deep breath in, then hum as you breathe out, again for as long as you can. Time the hum.

3. Try the same while whispering your favourite song, then again when singing.

246 At the top of the windpipe, making a bulge at the front of the neck, is the voice-box or larynx. It has two stiff flaps, vocal cords, which stick out from its sides. Normally these flaps are apart for easy breathing. But muscles in the voice-box can pull the flaps almost together. As air passes through the narrow slit between them it makes the flaps shake or vibrate — and this is the sound of your voice.

▼ The vocal cords are held apart for breathing (left) and pulled together for speech (right).

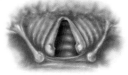
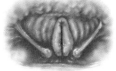

Breathing parts

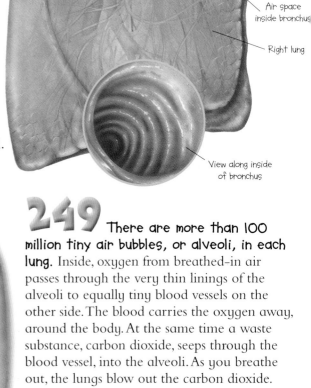

247 The main parts of the respiratory (breathing) system are the two lungs in the chest. Each one is shaped like a tall cone, with the pointed end at shoulder level.

248 Air comes in and out of the lungs along the windpipe, which branches at its base to form two main air tubes, the bronchi. One goes to each lung. Inside the lung, each bronchus divides again and again, becoming narrower each time. Finally the air tubes, thinner than hairs, end at groups of tiny 'bubbles' called alveoli.

Left bronchus

Muscles in wa of bronchus

Air space inside bronchus

Right lung

View along inside of bronchus

I DON'T BELIEVE IT!

On average, the air breathed in and out through the night by a sleeping person, would fill an average–sized bedroom. This is why some people like to sleep with the door or window open!

249 There are more than 100 million tiny air bubbles, or alveoli, in each lung. Inside, oxygen from breathed–in air passes through the very thin linings of the alveoli to equally tiny blood vessels on the other side. The blood carries the oxygen away, around the body. At the same time a waste substance, carbon dioxide, seeps through the blood vessel, into the alveoli. As you breathe out, the lungs blow out the carbon dioxide.

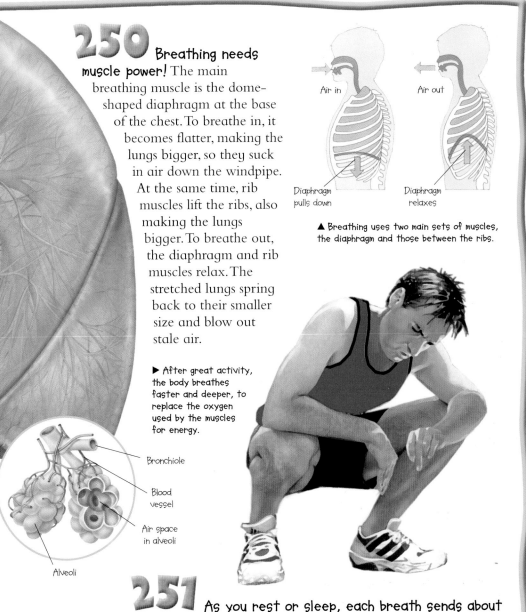

250 Breathing needs muscle power! The main breathing muscle is the dome-shaped diaphragm at the base of the chest. To breathe in, it becomes flatter, making the lungs bigger, so they suck in air down the windpipe. At the same time, rib muscles lift the ribs, also making the lungs bigger. To breathe out, the diaphragm and rib muscles relax. The stretched lungs spring back to their smaller size and blow out stale air.

Air in

Air out

Diaphragm pulls down

Diaphragm relaxes

▲ Breathing uses two main sets of muscles, the diaphragm and those between the ribs.

▶ After great activity, the body breathes faster and deeper, to replace the oxygen used by the muscles for energy.

Bronchiole

Blood vessel

Air space in alveoli

Alveoli

▲ Inside each lung, the main bronchus divides again and again, into thousands of narrower airways called bronchioles.

251 As you rest or sleep, each breath sends about half a litre of air in and out, 15 to 20 times each minute. After great activity, such as running a race, you need more oxygen. So you take deeper breaths faster – 3 litres or more of air, 50 times or more each minute.

The hungry body

252 **All machines need fuel to make them go, and the body is like a living machine whose fuel is food.** Food gives us energy for our body processes inside, and for breathing, moving, talking and every other action we make. Food also provides raw materials that the body uses to grow, maintain itself and repair daily wear-and-tear.

▶ Fish, low-fat meats like chicken, and dairy produce such as eggs all contain plenty of valuable proteins.

▶ Foods such as bread, pasta and rice contain lots of starch, which is a useful energy source.

253 **We would not put the wrong fuel into a car engine, so we should not put unsuitable foods into the body.** A healthy diet needs a wide variety of different foods, especially fresh vegetables and fruits, which have lots of vital nutrients. Too much of one single food may be unhealthy, especially if that food is very fatty or greasy. Too much of all foods is also unhealthy. It makes the body overweight, which increases the risk of various illnesses.

▶ Cheeses, and fatty and oily foods, are needed in moderate amounts. Plant oils are healthier than fats and oils from animal sources.

254 There are six main kinds of nutrients in foods, and the body needs balanced amounts of all of them.

• Proteins are needed for growth and repair, and for strong muscles and other parts.

• Carbohydrates, such as sugars and starches, give plenty of energy.

• Some fats are important for general health and energy.

• Vitamins help the body to fight germs and disease.

• Minerals are needed for strong bones and teeth and also healthy blood.

• Fibre is important for good digestion and to prevent certain bowel disorders.

▲ Fresh fruits such as bananas, and vegetables such as carrots, have lots of vitamins, minerals and fibre, and are good for the body in lots of ways.

FOOD FOR THOUGHT

Which of these meals do you think is healthier?

Meal A
Burger, sausage and lots of chips, followed by ice-cream with cream and chocolate.

Meal B
Chicken, tomato and a few chips, followed by fresh fruit salad with apple, banana, pear and melon.

Answer:
Meal B

115

Bite, chew, gulp

255 The hardest parts of your whole body are the ones that make holes in your food — teeth. They have a covering of whitish or yellowish enamel, which is stronger than most kinds of rocks! Teeth need to last a lifetime of biting, nibbling, gnashing, munching and chewing. They are your own food processors.

256 There are four main shapes of teeth. The front ones are incisors, and each has a straight, sharp edge, like a spade or chisel, to cut through food. Next are canines, which are taller and more pointed, used mainly for tearing and pulling. Behind them are premolars and molars, which are lower and flatter with small bumps, for crushing and grinding.

257 A tooth may look almost dead, but it is very much alive. Under the enamel is slightly softer dentine. In the middle of the tooth is the dental pulp. This has blood vessels to nourish the whole tooth, and nerves that feel pressure, heat, cold and pain. The lower part of the tooth, strongly fixed in the jaw bone, is the root. The enamel-covered part above the gum is the crown.

▶ At the centre of a tooth is living pulp, with many blood vessels and nerve endings that pass into the jaw bone.

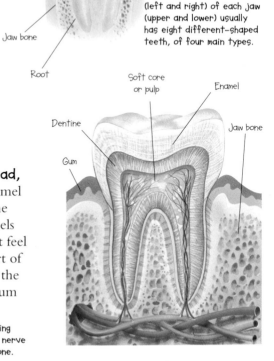

Incisor

Canine

Premolar

Molar

Jaw bone

Root

▲ In an adult, each side (left and right) of each jaw (upper and lower) usually has eight different-shaped teeth, of four main types.

Soft core or pulp

Enamel

Dentine

Jaw bone

Gum

258 Teeth are very strong and tough, but they do need to be cleaned properly and regularly. Germs called bacteria live on old bits of food in the mouth. They make waste products which are acid and eat into the enamel and dentine, causing holes called cavities. Which do you prefer – cleaning your teeth after main meals and before bedtime, or the agony of toothache?

▶ Clean your teeth by brushing in different directions and then flossing between them. They will look better and stay healthier for longer.

▼ The first set of teeth lasts about ten years, while the second set can last ten times longer.

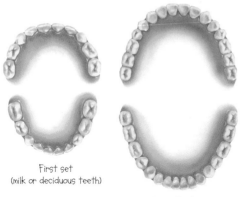

First set
(milk or deciduous teeth)

Second set
(adult or permanent set)

259 Teeth are designed to last a lifetime. Well, not quite, because the body has two sets. There are 20 small teeth in the first or baby set. The first ones usually appear above the gum by about six months of age, the last ones at three years old. As you and your mouth grow, the baby teeth fall out from about seven years old. They are replaced by 32 larger teeth in the adult set.

260 After chewing, food is swallowed into the gullet (oesophagus). This pushes the food powerfully down through the chest, past the heart and lungs, into the stomach.

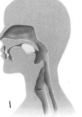

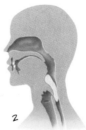

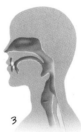

1

2

3

tongue pushes food to the back of the throat

throat muscles squeeze the food downwards

the oesophagus pushes food to the stomach

Food's long journey

261 The digestive system is like a tunnel about 9 metres long, through the body. It includes parts of the body that bite food, chew it, swallow it, churn it up and break it down with natural juices and acids, take in its goodness, and then get rid of the leftovers.

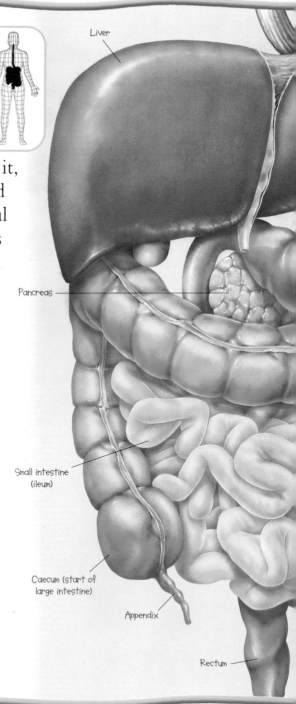

Liver

Pancreas

Small intestine (ileum)

Caecum (start of large intestine)

Appendix

Rectum

262 The stomach is a bag with strong, muscular walls. It stretches as it fills with food and drink, and its lining makes powerful digestive acids and juices called enzymes, to attack the food. The muscles in its walls squirm and squeeze to mix the food and juices.

263 The stomach digests food for a few hours into a thick mush, which oozes into the small intestine. This is only 4 centimetres wide, but more than 5 metres long. It takes nutrients and useful substances through its lining, into the body.

264 The large intestine follows the small one, and it is certainly wider, at about 6 centimetres, but much shorter, only 1.5 metres. It takes in fluids and a few more nutrients from the food, and then squashes what's left into brown lumps, ready to leave the body.

Stomach

Large intestine

▶ The lining of the small intestine has thousands of tiny finger-like parts called the villi, which take nutrients from food, into the blood and lymph system.

◀ The digestive parts almost fill the lower part of the main body, called the abdomen.

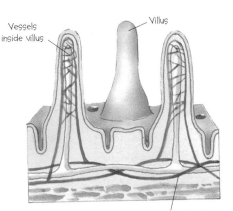

Vessels inside villus

Villus

Vessels in intestine lining

265 The liver and pancreas are also parts of the digestive system. The liver sorts out and changes the many nutrients from digestion, and stores some of them. The pancreas makes powerful digestive juices that pass to the small intestine to work on the food there.

I DON'T BELIEVE IT!

What's in the leftovers? The brown lumps called bowel motions or faeces are only about one-half undigested or leftover food. Some of the rest is rubbed-off parts of the stomach and intestine lining. The rest is millions of 'friendly' but dead microbes (bacteria) from the intestine. They help to digest our food for us, and in return we give them a warm, food-filled place to live.

Blood in the body

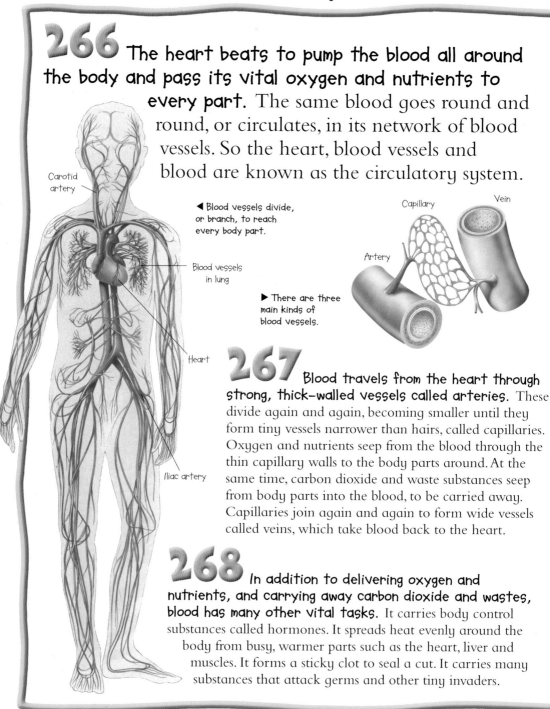

266 The heart beats to pump the blood all around the body and pass its vital oxygen and nutrients to every part. The same blood goes round and round, or circulates, in its network of blood vessels. So the heart, blood vessels and blood are known as the circulatory system.

Carotid artery

◀ Blood vessels divide, or branch, to reach every body part.

Blood vessels in lung

Capillary

Vein

Artery

▶ There are three main kinds of blood vessels.

Heart

267 Blood travels from the heart through strong, thick-walled vessels called arteries. These divide again and again, becoming smaller until they form tiny vessels narrower than hairs, called capillaries. Oxygen and nutrients seep from the blood through the thin capillary walls to the body parts around. At the same time, carbon dioxide and waste substances seep from body parts into the blood, to be carried away. Capillaries join again and again to form wide vessels called veins, which take blood back to the heart.

Iliac artery

268 In addition to delivering oxygen and nutrients, and carrying away carbon dioxide and wastes, blood has many other vital tasks. It carries body control substances called hormones. It spreads heat evenly around the body from busy, warmer parts such as the heart, liver and muscles. It forms a sticky clot to seal a cut. It carries many substances that attack germs and other tiny invaders.

269

Blood has four main parts. The largest is billions of tiny, saucer-shaped red cells, which make up almost half of the total volume of blood and carry oxygen. Second is the white cells, which clean the blood, prevent disease and fight germs. The third part is billions of tiny platelets, which help blood to clot. Fourth is watery plasma, in which the other parts float.

QUIZ

Can you match these blood parts and vessels with their descriptions?
a. Artery b. Vein c. White blood cell
d. Red blood cell e. Platelet f. Capillary

1. Large vessel that takes blood back to the heart
2. Tiny vessel allowing oxygen and nutrients to leave blood
3. Large vessel carrying blood away from the heart
4. Oxygen-carrying part of the blood
5. Disease-fighting part of the blood
6. Part that helps blood to clot

Answers:
a3 b1 c5 d4 c6 f2

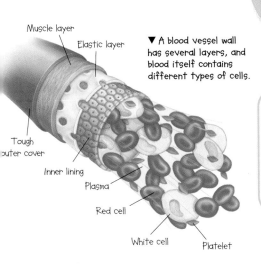

Muscle layer
Elastic layer
Tough outer cover
Inner lining
Plasma
Red cell
White cell
Platelet

▼ A blood vessel wall has several layers, and blood itself contains different types of cells.

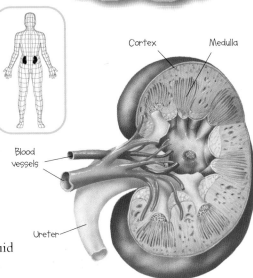

Cortex
Medulla
Blood vessels
Ureter

270

Blood is cleaned by two kidneys, situated in the middle of your back. They filter the blood and make a liquid called urine, which contains unwanted and waste substances, plus excess or 'spare' water. The urine trickles from each kidney down a tube, the ureter, into a stretchy bag, the bladder. It's stored here until you can get rid of it – at your convenience.

▲ Each kidney has about one million tiny filters, called nephrons, in its outer layer, or cortex.

The beating body

271 **The heart is about as big as its owner's clenched fist.** It is a hollow bag of very strong muscle, called cardiac muscle or myocardium. This muscle never tires. It contracts once every second or more often, all through life. The contraction, or heartbeat, squeezes blood inside the heart out into the arteries. As the heart relaxes it fills again with blood from the veins.

272 **Inside, the heart is not one baglike pump, but two pumps side by side.** The left pump sends blood all around the body, from head to toe, to deliver its oxygen (systemic circulation). The blood comes back to the right pump and is sent to the lungs, to collect more oxygen (pulmonary circulation). The blood returns to the left pump and starts the whole journey again.

▶ The heart is two pumps side by side, and each pump has two chambers, the upper atrium and the lower ventricle.

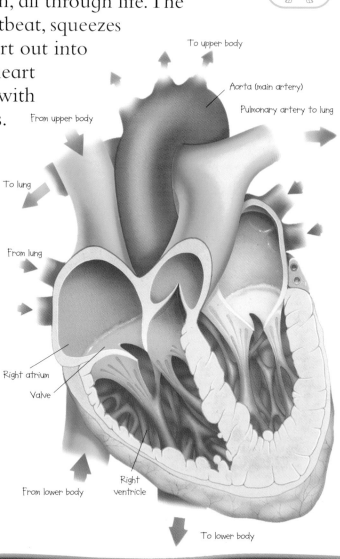

To upper body

Aorta (main artery)

Pulmonary artery to lung

From upper body

To lung

From lung

Right atrium

Valve

From lower body

Right ventricle

To lower body

273 Inside the heart are four sets of bendy flaps called valves. These open to let blood flow the right way. If the blood tries to move the wrong way, it pushes the flaps together and the valve closes. Valves make sure the blood flows the correct way, rather than sloshing to and fro, in and out of the heart, with each beat.

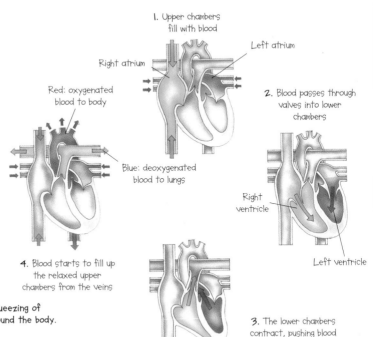

I. Upper chambers fill with blood

Left atrium

Right atrium

Red: oxygenated blood to body

2. Blood passes through valves into lower chambers

Blue: deoxygenated blood to lungs

Right ventricle

Left ventricle

4. Blood starts to fill up the relaxed upper chambers from the veins

3. The lower chambers contract, pushing blood into the arteries

▶ The heartbeat is the regular squeezing of the heart muscle to pump blood around the body.

274 The heart is the body's most active part, and it needs plenty of energy brought by the blood. The blood flows through small vessels, which branch across its surface and down into its thick walls. These are called the coronary vessels.

275 The heart beats at different rates, depending on what the body is doing. When the muscles are active they need more energy and oxygen, brought by the blood. So the heart beats faster, 120 times each minute or more. At rest, the heart slows to 60 to 80 beats per minute.

HOW FAST IS YOUR HEARTBEAT?

You will need:
plastic funnel   tracing paper
plastic tube (like hosepipe)   sticky-tape

You can hear your heart and count its beats with a sound-funnel device called a stethoscope.

1. Stretch the tracing paper over the funnel's wide end and tape in place. Push a short length of tube over the funnel's narrow end.

2. Place the funnel's wide end over your heart, on your chest, just to the left, and put the tube end to your ear. Listen to and count your heartbeat.

Looking and listening

276 The body finds out about the world around it by its senses – and the main sense is eyesight. The eyes detect the brightness, colours and patterns of light rays, and change these into patterns of nerve signals that they send to the brain. More than half of the knowledge, information and memories stored in the brain come into the body through the eyes.

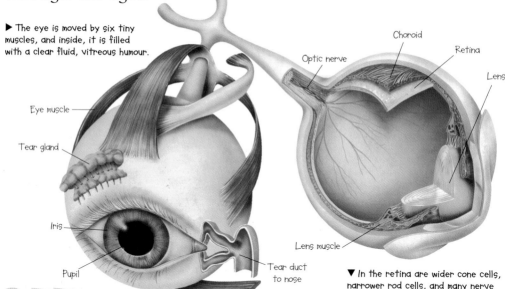

► The eye is moved by six tiny muscles, and inside, it is filled with a clear fluid, vitreous humour.

Choroid

Retina

Optic nerve

Lens

Eye muscle

Tear gland

Iris

Pupil

Lens muscle

Tear duct to nose

277 Each eye is a ball about 2.5 centimetres across. At the front is a clear dome, the cornea, which lets light through a small, dark-looking hole just behind it, the pupil. The light then passes through a pea-shaped lens which bends the rays so they shine a clear picture onto the inside back of the eye, the retina. This has 125 million tiny cells, rods and cones, which detect the light and make nerve signals to send along the optic nerve to the brain.

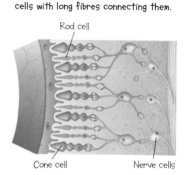

▼ In the retina are wider cone cells, narrower rod cells, and many nerve cells with long fibres connecting them.

Rod cell

Cone cell

Nerve cells

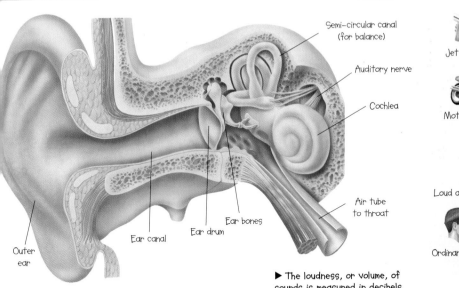

Semi-circular canal
(for balance)

Auditory nerve

Cochlea

Jet engine 130 dB

Motorcycle 100 dB

Air tube
to throat

Loud appliance 75 dB

Ear bones

Ear drum

Ear canal

Ordinary speech 60 dB

Outer
ear

▶ The loudness, or volume, of
sounds is measured in decibels
(dB). Louder than about 90 dB
can damage hearing.

Whisper 20 dB

▲ Most of the small,
delicate parts of the
ear are inside the head,
well protected by skull
bones around them.

278

The ear is far more than the bendy, curly flap on the side of the head. The ear flap funnels sound waves along a short tunnel, the ear canal, to a fingernail-sized patch of tight skin, the eardrum. As sound waves hit the eardrum it shakes or vibrates, and passes the vibrations to a row of three tiny bones. These are the ear ossicles, the smallest bones in the body. They also vibrate and pass on the vibrations to another part, the cochlea, which has a curly, snail-like shape.

BRIGHT AND DIM

Look at your eyes in a mirror. See how the dark hole which lets in light, the pupil, is quite small. The coloured part around the pupil, the iris, is a ring of muscle.

se your eyes for a minute, then open them and k carefully. Does the pupil quickly get smaller?

ile the eyes were closed, the iris made the pupil gger, to try and let in more light, so you could try to see in the darkness. As you open your eyes, the iris makes the pupil smaller again, to prevent too much light from dazzling you.

279

Inside the cochlea, the vibrations pass through fluid and shake rows of thousands of tiny hairs which grow from specialized hair cells. As the hairs vibrate, the hair cells make nerve signals, which flash along the auditory nerve to the brain.

Smelling and tasting

▼ The parts that carry out smelling are in the roof of the large chamber inside the nose.

Olfactory cells

Mucus lining

Nasal cavity

280 You cannot see smells, which are tiny particles floating in the air – but your nose can smell them. Your nose is more sensitive than you realize. It can detect more than 10,000 different scents, odours, fragrances, pongs and niffs. Smell is useful because it warns us if food is bad or rotten, and perhaps dangerous to eat. That's why we sniff a new or strange food item, almost without thinking, before trying it.

▼ Olfactory (smell) cells have micro-hairs facing down into the nasal chamber, which detect smell particles landing on them.

281 Smell particles drift with breathed-in air into the nose and through the nasal chamber behind it. At the top of the chamber are two patches of lining, each about the area of a thumbnail and with 250 million microscopic hairs. The particles land on the sticky hairs, and if they fit into landing sites called receptors there, like a key into a lock, then nerve signals flash along the olfactory nerve to the brain.

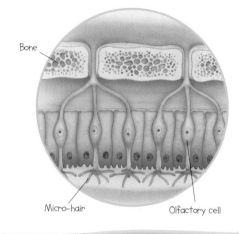

Bone

Micro-hair

Olfactory cell

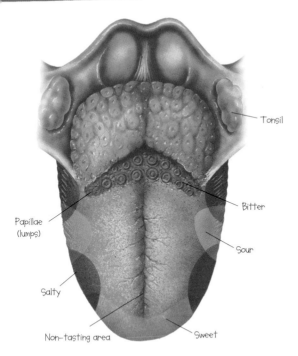

Tonsil

Bitter

Papillae
(lumps)

Sour

Salty

Non-tasting area

Sweet

282 The body's most flexible muscle is also the one which is coated with 10,000 micro-sensors for taste — the **tongue.** Each micro-sensor is a taste bud shaped like a tiny onion. Most taste buds are along the tip, sides and rear upper surface of the tongue. They are scattered around the much larger flaps and lumps on the tongue, which are called papillae.

◀ The taste buds are mainly around the edges of the tongue, not on the main middle area.

283 Taste works in a similar way to smell, but it detects flavour particles in foods and drinks. The particles touch tiny hairs sticking up from hair cells in the taste buds. If the particles fit into receptors there, then the hair cell makes nerve signals, which go along the facial and other nerves to the brain.

Taste bud

Cleft of papillus

Muscle of tongue

SWEET AND SOUR

The tongue detects only four basic flavours — sweet at the tip, salty along the front sides, sour along the rear sides, and bitter across the back.

Which of these foods is sweet, salty, bitter or sour?

1. Coffee 2. Lemon 3. Bacon
4. Ice cream

Answers:
1. bitter 2. sour 3. salty 4. sweet

◀ The large pimple-like lumps at the back of the tongue, called papillae, have tiny taste buds in their deep clefts.

The nervous body

Brain

Spinal cord

284 The body is not quite a 'bag of nerves', but it does contain thousands of kilometres of these pale, shiny threads. Nerves carry tiny electrical pulses known as nerve signals or neural messages. They form a vast information-sending network that reaches every part, almost like the body's own Internet.

Sciatic nerve

Tibial nerve

285 Each nerve is a bundle of much thinner parts called nerve fibres. Like wires in a telephone cable, these carry their own tiny electrical nerve signals. A typical nerve signal has a strength of 0.1 volts (one-fifteenth as strong as a torch battery). The slowest nerve signals travel about half a metre each second, the fastest at more than 100 metres per second.

Axon

▲ Nerves branch from the brain and spinal cord to every body part.

Dendrites

Synapse (junction between nerve cells)

286 All nerve signals are similar, but there are two main kinds, depending on where they are going. Sensory nerve signals travel from the sensory parts (eyes, ears, nose, tongue and skin) to the brain. Motor nerve signals travel from the brain out to the muscles, to make the body move about.

TIME TO REACT!

You will need:

friend   ruler

1. Ask your friend holds the ruler by the end with the highest measurement, letting it hang down. Put your thumb and fingers level with the other end, ready to grab.

2. Get your friend to let the ruler go, for you to grasp it as it falls. Measure where your thumb is on the ruler. Swap places so your friend has a go.

3. The person who grabs the ruler nearest its lower end has the fastest reactions. To grab the ruler, nerve signals travel from the eye, to the brain, and back out to the muscles in the arm and hand.

287 Hormones are part of the body's inner control system. A hormone is a chemical made by a gland. It travels in the blood and affects other body parts, for example, making them work faster or release more of their product.

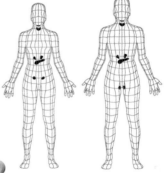

▼ Female and male bodies have much the same hormone-making glands, except for the reproductive parts – ovaries in the female (left) and testes in the male (right).

288 The main hormonal gland, the pituitary, is also the smallest. Just under the brain, it has close links with the nervous system. It mainly controls other hormonal glands. One is the thyroid in the neck, which affects the body's growth and how fast its chemical processes work. The pancreas controls how the body uses energy, by its hormone, insulin. The adrenal glands are involved in the body's balance of water, minerals and salts, and how we react to stress and fear.

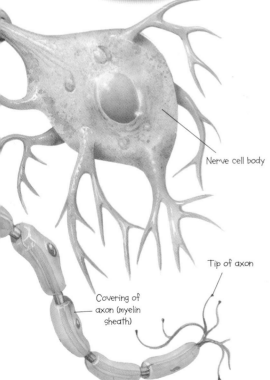

Nerve cell body

Tip of axon

Covering of axon (myelin sheath)

◄ The brain and nerves are made of billions of specialized cells, nerve cells or neurons. Each has many tiny branches, dendrites, to collect nerve messages, and a longer, thicker branch, the axon or fibre, to pass on the messages.

The brainy body

289 **Your brain is as big as your two fists side by side.** It's the place where you think, learn, work out problems, remember, feel happy and sad, wonder, worry, have ideas, sleep and dream.

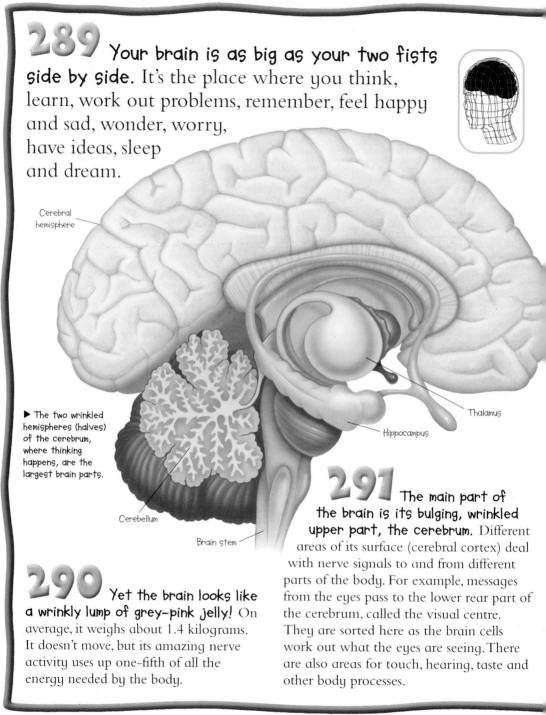

Cerebral hemisphere

▶ The two wrinkled hemispheres (halves) of the cerebrum, where thinking happens, are the largest brain parts.

Cerebellum

Brain stem

Thalamus

Hippocampus

291 **The main part of the brain is its bulging, wrinkled upper part, the cerebrum.** Different areas of its surface (cerebral cortex) deal with nerve signals to and from different parts of the body. For example, messages from the eyes pass to the lower rear part of the cerebrum, called the visual centre. They are sorted here as the brain cells work out what the eyes are seeing. There are also areas for touch, hearing, taste and other body processes.

290 **Yet the brain looks like a wrinkly lump of grey-pink jelly!** On average, it weighs about 1.4 kilograms. It doesn't move, but its amazing nerve activity uses up one-fifth of all the energy needed by the body.

292
The cerebellum is the rounded, wrinkled part at the back of the brain. It processes messages from the motor centre, sorting and coordinating them in great detail, to send to the body's hundreds of muscles. This is how we learn skilled, precise movements such as writing, skateboarding or playing music (or all three), almost without thinking.

293
The brain stem is the lower part of the brain, where it joins the body's main nerve, the spinal cord. The brain stem controls basic processes vital for life, like breathing, heartbeat, digesting food and removing wastes.

294
The brain really does have 'brain waves'. Every second it receives, sorts and sends millions of nerve signals. Special pads attached to the head can detect these tiny electrical pulses. They are shown on a screen or paper strip as wavy lines called an EEG, electro-encephalogram.

▼ Different areas or centres of the brain's outer layer, the cerebral cortex, deal with messages from and to certain parts of the body.

Touch area
Movement area
Thought area
Vision area
Hearing area
Speech area

▼ The brain's 'waves' or EEG recordings change, depending on whether the person is alert and thinking hard, resting, falling asleep or deeply asleep.

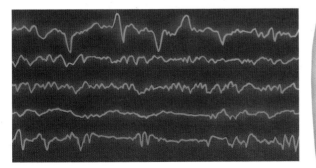

I DON'T BELIEVE IT!
The brain never sleeps! EEG waves show that it is almost as busy at night as when we are awake. It still controls heartbeat, breathing and digestion. It also sifts through the day's events and stores memories.

The healthy body

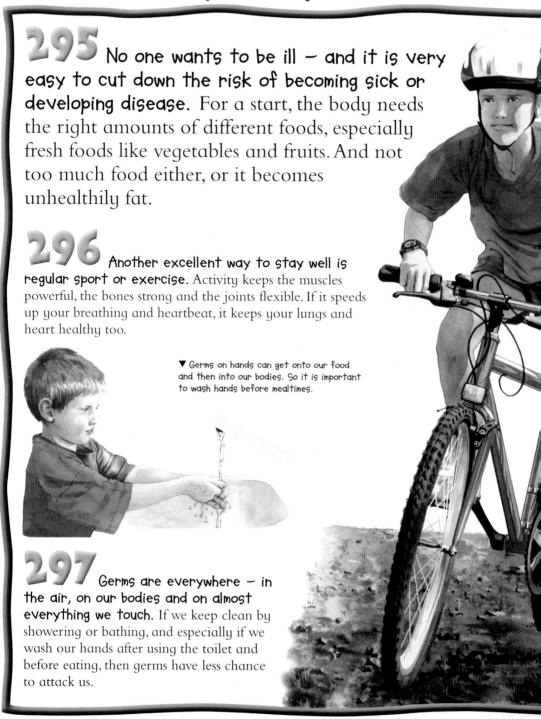

295 No one wants to be ill — and it is very easy to cut down the risk of becoming sick or developing disease. For a start, the body needs the right amounts of different foods, especially fresh foods like vegetables and fruits. And not too much food either, or it becomes unhealthily fat.

296 Another excellent way to stay well is regular sport or exercise. Activity keeps the muscles powerful, the bones strong and the joints flexible. If it speeds up your breathing and heartbeat, it keeps your lungs and heart healthy too.

▼ Germs on hands can get onto our food and then into our bodies. So it is important to wash hands before mealtimes.

297 Germs are everywhere — in the air, on our bodies and on almost everything we touch. If we keep clean by showering or bathing, and especially if we wash our hands after using the toilet and before eating, then germs have less chance to attack us.

298 **Health is not only in the body, it's in the mind.** Too much worry and stress can cause many illnesses, such as headaches and digestive upsets. This is why it's so important to talk about troubles and share them with someone who can help.

◀ Exercise keeps the body fit and healthy, and it should be fun too. It is always best to reduce risks of having an accident by wearing a cycle helmet for example.

▶ In some immunizations, dead versions of a germ are put into the body using a syringe, so the body can develop resistance to them without suffering from the disease they cause.

299 **Doctors and nurses help us to recover from sickness, and they also help prevent illness.** Regular check-ups at the dentist, optician and health centre are vital. For most people immunizations (vaccinations) also help to protect against diseases. It is good to report any health problem early, before they become too serious to treat.

300 **Old age is getting older!** More people live to be 100 years or more and for many of them, their bodies are still working well. How would you like to spend your 100th birthday?

What is weather?

301 **Rain, sunshine, snow and storms are all types of weather.** These help us decide what clothes we wear, what food we eat, and what kind of life we lead. Weather also affects how animals and plants survive. Different types of weather are caused by what is happening in the atmosphere, the air above our heads. In some parts of the world, the weather changes every day, in others, it is nearly always the same.

Equator

302 **Tropical, temperate and polar are all types of climate.** Climate is the name we give to patterns of weather over a period of time. Near the Equator, the weather is mostly hot and steamy. We call this a tropical climate. Near the North and South Poles, ice lies on the ground year-round and there are biting-cold blizzards. This is a polar climate. Most of the world has a temperate climate, with a mix of cold and warm seasons.

Tropical

Tropical forest

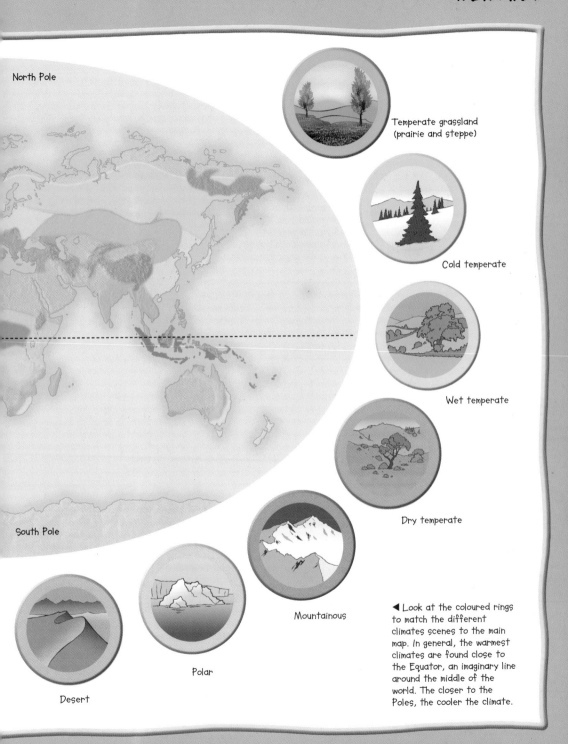

North Pole

Temperate grassland
(prairie and steppe)

Cold temperate

Wet temperate

Dry temperate

South Pole

Mountainous

Polar

Desert

◄ Look at the coloured rings
to match the different
climates scenes to the main
map. In general, the warmest
climates are found close to
the Equator, an imaginary line
around the middle of the
world. The closer to the
Poles, the cooler the climate.

The four seasons

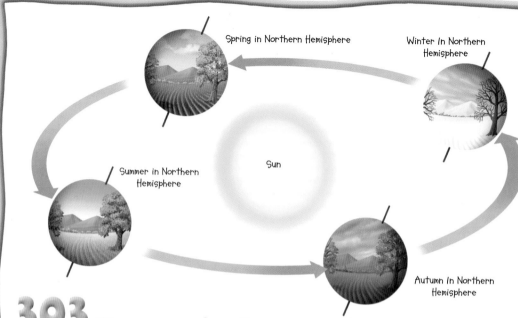

Spring in Northern Hemisphere

Winter In Northern Hemisphere

Sun

Summer in Northern Hemisphere

Autumn In Northern Hemisphere

303 The reason for the seasons lies in space.

Our planet Earth plots a path through space that takes it around the Sun. This path, or orbit, takes one year. The Earth is tilted, so over the year first one and then the other Pole leans towards the Sun, giving us seasons. In June, for example, the North Pole leans towards the Sun. The Sun heats the northern half of Earth and there is summer.

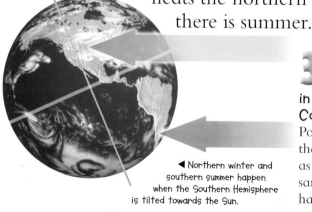

◄ Northern winter and southern summer happen when the Southern Hemisphere is tilted towards the Sun.

304 When it is summer in Argentina, it is winter in Canada.

In December, the South Pole leans towards the Sun. Places in the southern half of the world, such as Argentina, have summer. At the same time, places in the northern half, such as Canada, have winter.

305
A day can last 21 hours! Night and day happen because Earth is spinning as it circles the Sun. At the height of summer, places near the North Pole are so tilted towards the Sun that it is light almost all day long. In Stockholm, Sweden, Midsummer's Eve lasts 21 hours because the Sun disappears below the horizon for only three hours.

▲ At the North Pole, the Sun never disappears below the horizon at Midsummer's Day.

▼ Deciduous trees like these lose their leaves in autumn, but evergreens keep their leaves all year round.

I DON'T BELIEVE IT !
When the Sun shines all day in the far north, there is 24-hour night in the far south.

306
Forests change colour in the autumn. Autumn comes between summer and winter. Trees prepare for the cold winter months ahead by losing their leaves. First, though, they suck back the precious green chlorophyll, or dye, in their leaves, making them turn glorious shades of red, orange and brown.

Fewer seasons

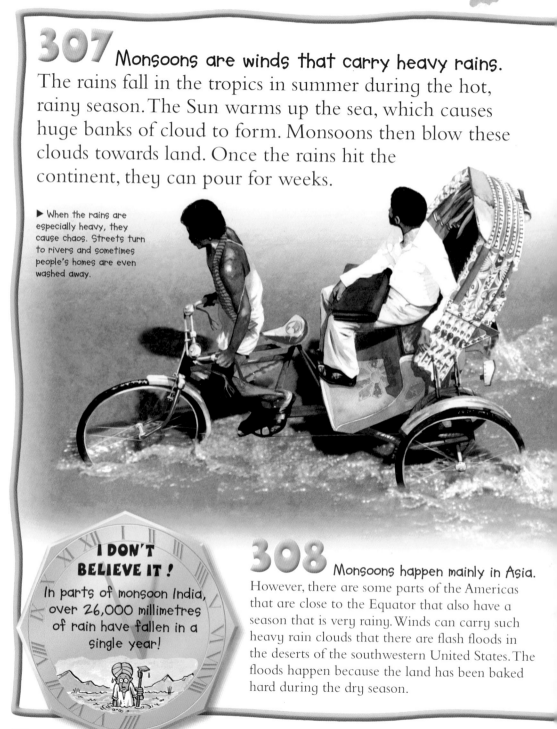

307 **Monsoons are winds that carry heavy rains.**
The rains fall in the tropics in summer during the hot,
rainy season. The Sun warms up the sea, which causes
huge banks of cloud to form. Monsoons then blow these
clouds towards land. Once the rains hit the
continent, they can pour for weeks.

▶ When the rains are
especially heavy, they
cause chaos. Streets turn
to rivers and sometimes
people's homes are even
washed away.

**I DON'T
BELIEVE IT !**

In parts of monsoon India,
over 26,000 millimetres
of rain have fallen in a
single year!

308 **Monsoons happen mainly in Asia.**
However, there are some parts of the Americas
that are close to the Equator that also have a
season that is very rainy. Winds can carry such
heavy rain clouds that there are flash floods in
the deserts of the southwestern United States. The
floods happen because the land has been baked
hard during the dry season.

309

Many parts of the tropics have two seasons, not four.
They are the parts of the world closest to the Equator, an imaginary line around the middle of the Earth. Here it is always hot, as these places are constantly facing the Sun. However, the movement of the Earth affects the position of a great band of cloud. In June, the tropical areas north of the Equator have the strongest heat and the heaviest rain storms. In December, it is the turn of the areas south of the Equator.

Tropic of Cancer

Equator

Tropic of Capricorn

▲ The tropics lie either side of the Equator, between lines of latitude called the Tropic of Cancer and the Tropic of Capricorn.

310

In a tropical rainforest, you need your umbrella every day! Rainforests have rainy weather all year round – but there is still a wet and a dry season. It is just that the wet season is even wetter!

▼ Daily rainfall feeds the lush rainforest vegetation.

What a scorcher!

311 All our heat comes from the Sun. The Sun is a star, a super-hot ball of burning gases. It gives off heat rays that travel 150 million kilometres through space to our planet. Over the journey, the rays cool down, but they can still scorch the Earth.

QUIZ

1. How many seasons are there in the tropics?

2. On which continent do most monsoons occur?

3. Where is the hottest recorded place in the world?

4. Is El Niño a wind or a current?

Answers:
1. Two 2. Asia
3. Al Aziziyah in Libya 4. A current

312 The Sahara is the sunniest place. This North African desert once had 4300 hours of sunshine in a year! People who live there, such as the Tuareg Arabs, cover their skin to avoid being sunburnt.

313 The hottest place on Earth is Al Aziziyah in Libya. It is 58°C in the shade – hot enough to fry an egg!

▶ Desert peoples wear headdresses to protect their skin and eyes from the sun and sand.

▼ A mirage is just a trick of the light. It can make us see something that is not really there.

314
The Sun can trick your eyes. Sometimes, as sunlight passes through our atmosphere, it hits layers of air at different temperatures. When this happens, the air bends the light and can trick our eyes into seeing something that is not there. This is a mirage. For example, what looks like a pool of water might really be part of the sky reflected on to the land.

315
Too much sun brings drought. Clear skies and sunshine are not always good news. Without rain crops wither, and people and their animals go hungry.

316
One terrible drought made a 'Dust Bowl'. Settlers in the American Mid-West were ruined by a long drought during the 1930s. As crops died, there were no roots to hold the soil together. The dry earth turned to dust and some farms simply blew away!

▲ The 'Dust Bowl' was caused by strong winds and dust storms. These destroyed huge areas of land.

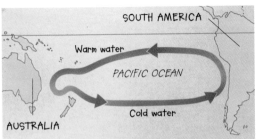

▲ El Niño has been known to cause violent weather conditions. It returns on average every four years.

317
A sea current can set forests alight. All sorts of things affect our weather and climate. The movements of a sea current called El Niño have been blamed for causing terrible droughts – which led to unstoppable forest fires.

Our atmosphere

318 Our planet is wrapped in a blanket of air. We call this blanket the atmosphere. It stretches hundreds of kilometres above our heads. The blanket keeps in heat, especially at night when part of the planet faces away from the Sun. During the day, the blanket becomes a sunscreen instead. Without an atmosphere, there would be no weather.

319 Most weather happens in the troposphere. This is the layer of atmosphere that stretches from the ground to around 10 kilometres above your head. The higher in the troposphere you go, the cooler the air. Because of this, clouds are most likely to form here. Clouds with flattened tops show just where the troposphere meets the next layer, the stratosphere.

KEY
1. Exosphere 190 to 960 kilometres
2. Thermosphere 80 to 190 kilometres
3. Mesosphere 50 to 80 kilometres
4. Stratosphere 10 to 50 kilometres
5. Troposphere 0 to 10 kilometres

◄ The atmosphere stretches right into space. Scientists have split it into five layers, or spheres, such as the troposphere.

320

Air just cannot keep still. Tiny particles in air, called molecules, are always bumping into each other! The more they smash into each other, the greater the air pressure. Generally, there are more smashes lower in the troposphere, because the pull of gravity makes the molecules fall towards the Earth's surface. The higher you go, the lower the air pressure, and the less oxygen there is in the air.

▶ At high altitudes there is less oxygen. That is why mountaineers often wear breathing equipment.

High pressure

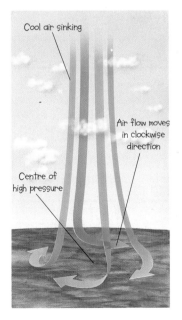

Cool air sinking

Air flow moves in clockwise direction

Centre of high pressure

Low pressure

Warm air rising

Air flow moves in anticlockwise direction

Centre of low pressure

321

Warmth makes air move. When heat from the Sun warms the molecules in air, they move faster and spread out more. This makes the air lighter, so it rises in the sky, creating low pressure. As it gets higher, the air cools. The molecules slow down and become heavier again, so they start to sink back to Earth.

◀ A high pressure weather system gives us warmer weather, while low pressure gives us cooler more unsettled weather.

Clouds and rain

322 Rain comes from the sea.

As the Sun heats the surface of the ocean, some seawater turns into water vapour and rises into the air. As it rises, it cools and turns back into water droplets. Lots of water droplets make clouds. The droplets join together to make bigger and bigger drops that eventually fall as rain. Some rain is soaked up by the land, but a lot finds its way back to the sea. This is called the water cycle.

RAIN GAUGE

You will need:

jam jar waterproof marker pen
ruler notebook pen

Put the jar outside. At the same time each day, mark the rainwater level on the jar with your pen. At the end of a week, empty the jar. Measure and record how much rain fell each day and over the whole week.

323 Some mountains are so tall that their summits (peaks) are hidden by cloud.

Really huge mountains even affect the weather. When moving air hits a mountain slope it is forced upwards. As it travels up, the temperature drops, and clouds form.

◀ Warm, rising air may be forced up the side of a mountain. At a certain level, lower temperatures make the water form clouds.

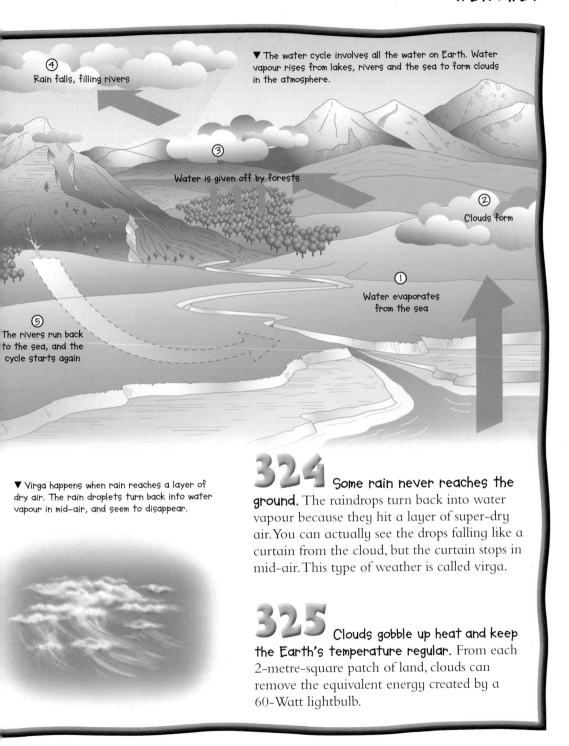

④ Rain falls, filling rivers

▼ The water cycle involves all the water on Earth. Water vapour rises from lakes, rivers and the sea to form clouds in the atmosphere.

③ Water is given off by forests

② Clouds form

① Water evaporates from the sea

⑤ The rivers run back to the sea, and the cycle starts again

▼ Virga happens when rain reaches a layer of dry air. The rain droplets turn back into water vapour in mid-air, and seem to disappear.

324 **Some rain never reaches the ground.** The raindrops turn back into water vapour because they hit a layer of super-dry air. You can actually see the drops falling like a curtain from the cloud, but the curtain stops in mid-air. This type of weather is called virga.

325 **Clouds gobble up heat and keep the Earth's temperature regular.** From each 2-metre-square patch of land, clouds can remove the equivalent energy created by a 60-Watt lightbulb.

Not just fluffy

326 **Clouds come in all shapes and sizes.** To help recognize them, scientists split them into ten basic types. The type depends on what the cloud looks like and where it forms in the sky. Cirrus clouds look like wisps of smoke. They form high in the troposphere and rarely mean rain. Stratus clouds form in flat layers and may produce drizzle or a sprinkling of snow. All types of cumulus clouds bring rain. Some are huge cauliflower shapes. They look soft and fluffy – but would feel soggy to touch.

Cumulonimbus clouds give heavy rain showers

▶ The main classes of cloud – cirrus, cumulus and stratus – were named in the 1800s. An amateur British weather scientist called Luke Howard identified the different types.

327 **Not all clouds produce rain.** Cumulus humilis clouds are the smallest heap-shaped clouds. In the sky, they look like lumpy, cotton wool sausages! They are too small to produce rain but they can grow into much bigger, rain-carrying cumulus clouds. The biggest cumulus clouds, cumulus congestus, bring heavy showers.

Cumulus clouds bring rain

Cirrus clouds occur at great heights from the ground

Cirrostratus

Contrails are the white streaks created by planes

329 Not all clouds are made by nature. Contrails are streaky clouds that a plane leaves behind it as it flies. They are made of water vapour that comes from the plane's engines. The second it hits the cold air, the vapour turns into ice crystals, leaving a trail of white snow cloud.

328 Sometimes the sky is filled with white patches of cloud that look like shimmering fish scales. These are called mackerel skies. It takes lots of gusty wind to break the cloud into these little patches, and so mackerel skies are usually a sign of changeable weather.

Stratus clouds can bring drizzle or appear as fog

MIX AND MATCH

Can you match the names of these five types of clouds to their meanings?

1. Altostratus   a. heap
2. Cirrus   b. layer
3. Cumulonimbus   c. high + layer
4. Cumulus   d. wisp
5. Stratus   e. heap + rain

Answers:
1.C 2.D 3.E
4.A 5.B

Flood warning

330 **Too much rain brings floods.** There are two different types of floods. Flash floods happen after a short burst of heavy rainfall, usually caused by thunderstorms. Broadscale flooding happens when rain falls steadily over a wide area – for weeks or months – without stopping. When this happens, rivers slowly fill and eventually burst their banks. Tropical storms, such as hurricanes, can also lead to broadscale flooding.

▲ Flooding can cause great damage to buildings and the countryside.

331 **There can be floods in the desert.** When a lot of rain falls very quickly on to land that has been baked dry, it cannot soak in. Instead, it sits on the surface, causing flash floods.

◀ A desert flash flood can create streams of muddy brown water. After the water level falls, vegetation bursts into life.

332

There really was a Great Flood. The Bible tells of a terrible flood, and how a man called Noah was saved. Recently, explorers found the first real evidence of the Flood – a sunken beach 140 metres below the surface of the Black Sea. There are ruins of houses, dating back to 5600BC. Stories of a huge flood in ancient times do not appear only in the Bible – the Babylonians and Greeks told of one, too.

▲ In the Bible story, Noah survived the Great Flood by building a huge wooden boat called an ark.

333

Mud can flood. When rain mixes with earth it makes mud. On bare mountainsides, there are no tree roots to hold the soil together. An avalanche of mud can slide off the mountain. The worst ever mudslide happened after flooding in Colombia, South America in 1985. It buried 23,000 people from the town of Armero.

▼ Mudslides can devastate whole towns and villages, as the flow of mud covers everything it meets.

I DON'T BELIEVE IT!

The ancient Egyptians had a story to explain the yearly flooding of the Nile. They said the goddess Isis filled the river with tears, as she cried for her lost husband.

Deep freeze

334 Snow is made of tiny ice crystals. When air temperatures are very cold – around 0°C – the water droplets in the clouds freeze to make tiny ice crystals. Sometimes, individual crystals fall, but usually they clump together into snowflakes.

336 Black ice is not really black. Drizzle or rain turns to ice when it touches freezing-cold ground. This 'black' ice is see-through, and hard to spot against a road's dark tarmac. It is also terribly slippery – like a deadly ice rink.

I DON'T BELIEVE IT!

Antarctica is the coldest place on Earth. Temperatures of −89.2°C have been recorded there.

▲ Falling snow is made worse by strong winds, which can form deep drifts.

335 No two snowflakes are the same. This is because snowflakes are made up of ice crystals, and every ice crystal is as unique as your fingerprint. Most crystals look like six-pointed stars, but they come in other shapes too.

▶ Ice crystals seen under a microscope. A snowflake that is several centimetres across will be made up of lots of crystals like these.

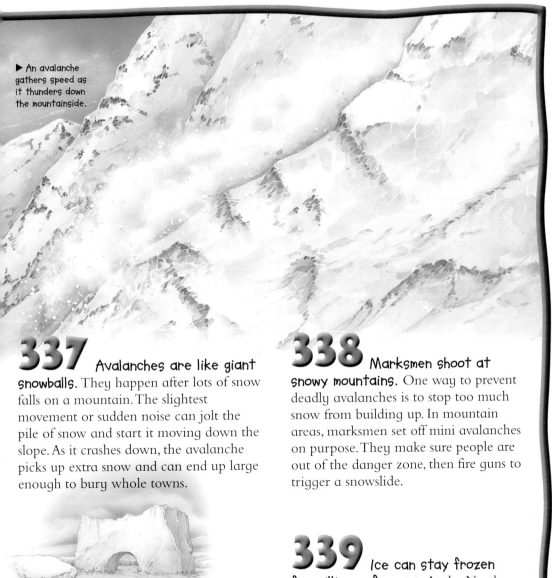

▶ An avalanche gathers speed as it thunders down the mountainside.

337
Avalanches are like giant snowballs. They happen after lots of snow falls on a mountain. The slightest movement or sudden noise can jolt the pile of snow and start it moving down the slope. As it crashes down, the avalanche picks up extra snow and can end up large enough to bury whole towns.

▲ Antarctica is a frozen wilderness. The ice piles up to form amazing shapes, like this arch.

338
Marksmen shoot at snowy mountains. One way to prevent deadly avalanches is to stop too much snow from building up. In mountain areas, marksmen set off mini avalanches on purpose. They make sure people are out of the danger zone, then fire guns to trigger a snowslide.

339
Ice can stay frozen for millions of years. At the North and South Poles, the weather never warms up enough for the ice to thaw. When fresh snow falls, it presses down on the snow already there, forming thick sheets. Some ice may not have melted for a million years or more.

When the wind blows

340
Wind is moving air. Winds blow because air is constantly moving from areas of high pressure to areas of low pressure. The bigger the difference in temperature between the two areas, the faster the wind blows.

▶ These trees have been forced into strange shapes by the wind.

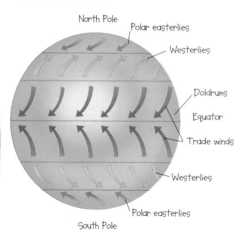

North Pole
Polar easterlies
Westerlies
Doldrums
Equator
Trade winds
Westerlies
Polar easterlies
South Pole

▲ This map shows the pattern of the world's main winds.

341
Trade winds blow one way north of the Equator, and another way in the south. Trade winds blow in the tropics, where air is moving to an area of low pressure at the Equator. Their name comes from their importance to traders, when goods travelled by sailing ship.

342
Winds have names. World wind patterns are called global winds. The most famous are the trade winds that blow towards the Equator. There are also well-known local winds, such as the cold, dry mistral that blows down to southern France, or the hot, dry sirroco that blows north of the Sahara.

QUIZ
1. At what temperature does water freeze?
2. What does the Beaufort Scale measure?
3. What are the mistral and sirroco?
4. How many sides does an ice crystal usually have?

Answers:
1. 0°C. 2. Wind strength
3. Local winds 4. Six

343

You can tell how windy it is by looking at the leaves on a tree. Wind ranges from light breezes to hurricanes. Its strength is measured on the Beaufort Scale, named after the Irish admiral who devised it. The scale ranges from Force 0, meaning total calm, to Force 12, which is a hurricane.

▶ The Beaufort Scale.

Force 0: Calm

Force 1: Light air

Force 2: Light breeze

Force 3: Gentle breeze

Force 4: Moderate breeze

Force 5: Fresh breeze

Force 6: Strong breeze

Force 7: Near gale

Force 8: Gale

Force 9: Strong gale

Force 10: Storm

Force 11: Violent storm

Force 12: Hurricane

▲ Turbines convert the wind's energy into electrical energy.

344

Wind can turn on your TV. People can harness the energy of the wind to make electricity for our homes. Tall turbines are positioned in windy spots. As the wind turns the turbine, the movement powers a generator and produces electrical energy.

345

Wind can make you mad! The Föhn wind, which blows across Switzerland, Austria and Bavaria in southern Germany, brings with it changeable weather. This has been blamed for road accidents and even bouts of madness!

Thunderbolts and lightning

346 **Thunderstorms are most likely in summer.** Hot weather creates warm, moist air that rises and forms towering cumulonimbus clouds. Inside each cloud, water droplets and ice crystals bang about, building up positive and negative electrical charges. Electricity flows between the charges, creating a flash that heats the air around it. Lightning is so hot that it makes the air expand, making a loud noise or thunderclap.

▼ Cloud—to—cloud lightning is called sheet lightning, while lightning travelling from the cloud to the ground is called fork lightning.

347
Lightning comes in different colours. If there is rain in the thundercloud, the lightning looks red; if there's hail, it looks blue. Lightning can also be yellow or white.

▼ Lightning conductors absorb the shock and protect tall buildings.

▶ Dramatic lightning flashes light up the sky.

348
Tall buildings are protected from lightning. Church steeples and other tall structures are often struck by bolts of lightning. This could damage the building, or give electric shocks to people inside, so lightning conductors are placed on the roof. These channel the lightning safely away.

349
A person can survive a lightning strike. Lightning is very dangerous and can give a big enough shock to kill you. However, an American park ranger called Roy Sullivan survived being struck seven times.

HOW CLOSE?

Lightning and thunder happen at the same time, but light travels faster than sound. Count the seconds between the flash and the clap and divide them by three. This is how many kilometres away the storm is.

▼ A sudden hail storm can leave the ground littered with small chunks of ice.

350
Hailstones can be as big as melons! These chunks of ice can fall from thunderclouds. The biggest ever fell in Gopaljang, Bangladesh, in 1986 and weighed 1 kilogram each!

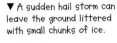

Eye of the hurricane

351 Some winds travel at speeds of more than 120 kilometres an hour. Violent tropical storms happen when strong winds blow into an area of low pressure and start spinning very fast. They develop over warm seas and pick up speed until they reach land, where there is no more moist sea air to feed them. Such storms bring torrential rain.

▼ A Hurricane Hunter heads into the storm.

352 The centre of a hurricane is calm and still. This part is called the 'eye'. As the eye of the storm passes over, there is a pause in the terrifying rains and wind.

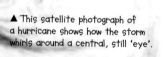

▲ This satellite photograph of a hurricane shows how the storm whirls around a central, still 'eye'.

353 Hurricane Hunters fly close to the eye of a hurricane. These are special weather planes that fly into the storm in order to take measurements. It is a dangerous job for the pilots, but the information they gather helps to predict the hurricane's path – and saves lives.

▲ A hurricane brings battering rain and massive waves.

354 **Hurricanes have names.** One of the worst hurricanes was Hurricane Andrew, which battered the coast of Florida in 1992. Perhaps there is a hurricane named after you!

355 **Hurricanes whip up wild waves.** As the storm races over the ocean, the winds create giant waves. These hit the shore as a huge sea surge. In 1961, the sea surge following Hurricane Hattie washed away Belize City in South America.

356 **Typhoons saved the Japanese from Genghis Khan.** The 13th-century Mongol leader made two attempts to invade Japan – and both times, a terrible typhoon battered his fleet and saved the Japanese!

▶ A typhoon prevented Genghis Khan's navy from invading Japan.

Wild whirling winds

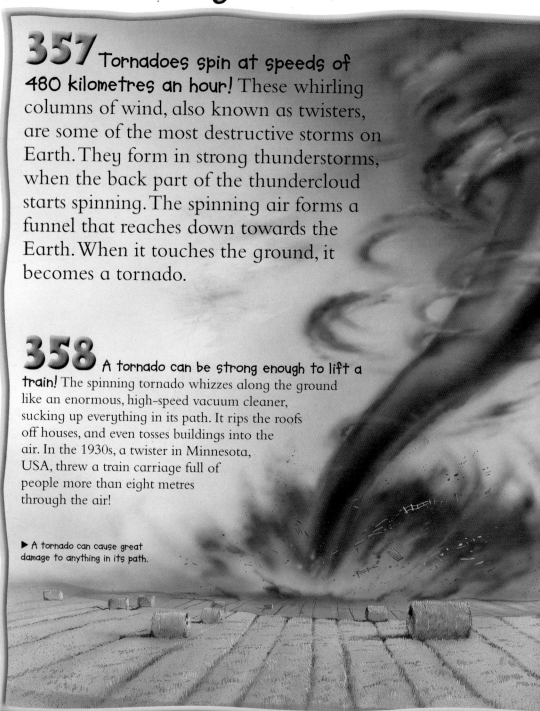

357 **Tornadoes spin at speeds of 480 kilometres an hour!** These whirling columns of wind, also known as twisters, are some of the most destructive storms on Earth. They form in strong thunderstorms, when the back part of the thundercloud starts spinning. The spinning air forms a funnel that reaches down towards the Earth. When it touches the ground, it becomes a tornado.

358 **A tornado can be strong enough to lift a train!** The spinning tornado whizzes along the ground like an enormous, high-speed vacuum cleaner, sucking up everything in its path. It rips the roofs off houses, and even tosses buildings into the air. In the 1930s, a twister in Minnesota, USA, threw a train carriage full of people more than eight metres through the air!

▶ A tornado can cause great damage to anything in its path.

359 Tornado Alley is a twister hotspot in the American Mid-West.

This is where hot air travelling north from the Gulf of Mexico meets cold polar winds travelling south, and creates huge thunderclouds. Of course, tornadoes can happen anywhere in the world when the conditions are right.

▲ The shaded area shows Tornado Alley, where there are hundreds of tornadoes each year.

360 A pillar of whirling water can rise out of a lake or the sea.

Waterspouts are spiralling columns of water that can be sucked up by a tornado as it forms over a lake or the sea. They tend to spin more slowly than tornadoes, because water is much heavier than air.

I DON'T BELIEVE IT !

Loch Ness in Scotland is famous for sightings of a monster nicknamed Nessie. Perhaps people who have seen Nessie were really seeing a waterspout.

▲ Waterspouts can suck up fish living in a lake!

▶ A whirling storm of sand in the desert.

361 Dust devils are desert tornadoes.

They shift tonnes of sand and cause terrible damage — they can strip the paintwork from a car in seconds!

Pretty lights

362 **Rainbows are made up of seven colours.** They are caused by sunlight passing through falling raindrops. The water acts like a glass prism, splitting the light. White light is made up of seven colours – red, orange, yellow, green, blue, indigo and violet – so these are the colours, from top to bottom, that make up the rainbow.

REMEMBER IT!

Richard Of York Gave Battle In Vain

The first letter of every word of this rhyme gives the first letter of each colour of the rainbow – as it appears in the sky:

Red Orange Yellow Green Blue Indigo Violet

363 **Two rainbows can appear at once.** The top rainbow is a reflection of the bottom one, so its colours appear the opposite way round, with the violet band at the top and red at the bottom.

364 **Some rainbows appear at night.** They happen when falling raindrops split moonlight, rather than sunlight. This sort of rainbow is called a moonbow.

▲ Although a fogbow is colourless, its inner edge may appear slightly blue and its outer edge slightly red.

365 It is not just angels that wear halos!

When you look at the Sun or Moon through a curtain of ice crystals, they seem to be surrounded by a glowing ring of light called a halo.

366 Three suns can appear in our sky!

'Mock suns' are two bright spots that appear on either side of the Sun. They often happen at the same time as a halo, and have the same cause – light passing through ice crystals in the air.

▼ An aurora – the most dazzling natural light show on Earth!

367 Some rainbows are just white.

Fogbows happen when sunlight passes through a patch of fog. The water droplets in the fog are too small to work like prisms, so the arching bow is white or colourless.

▲ A halo looks like a circle of light surrounding the Sun or Moon.

▲ Mock suns are also known as parhelia or sundogs.

368 Auroras are curtains of lights in the sky.

They happen in the far north or south of the world when particles from the Sun smash into molecules in the air – at speeds of 1600 kilometres an hour. The lights may be blue, red or yellow.

Made for weather

369 **Camels can go for two weeks without a drink.** They are adapted to life in a hot, dry climate. Camels do not sweat until their body temperature hits 40°C, which helps them to save water. Their humps are fat stores, which are used for energy when food and drink is scarce.

▼ These animals have adapted to life in very dry climates. However, they live in different deserts around the world.

370 **Lizards lose salt through their noses.** Most animals get rid of excess salt in their urine, but lizards, such as iguanas and geckos, live in dry parts of the world. They need to lose as little water from their bodies as possible.

Camels

Iguana

371 **Even toads can survive in the desert.** The spadefoot toad copes with desert conditions by staying underground in a burrow for most of the year. It only comes to the surface after a shower of rain.

Banded gecko

▶ Beneath its gleaming-white fur, the polar bear's skin is black to absorb heat from the Sun.

372 Polar bears have black skin.

These bears have all sorts of special ways to survive the polar climate. Plenty of body fat and thick fur keeps them snug and warm, while their black skin soaks up as much warmth from the Sun as possible.

373 Acorn woodpeckers store nuts for winter.

Animals in temperate climates have to be prepared if they are to survive the cold winter months. Acorn woodpeckers turn tree trunks into larders. During autumn, when acorns are ripe, the birds collect as many as they can, storing them in holes that they bore into a tree.

▶ Storing acorns helps this woodpecker survive the cold winter months.

Spadefoot toad

Weather myths

374 **People once thought the Sun was a god.** The sun god was often considered to be the most important god of all, because he brought light and warmth and ripened crops. The ancient Egyptians built pyramids that pointed up to their sun god, Re, while the Aztecs believed that their sun god, Huitzilpochtli, had even shown them where to build their capital city.

375 **The Vikings thought a god brought thunder.** Thor was the god of war and thunder, worshipped across what is now Scandinavia. The Vikings pictured Thor as a red-bearded giant. He carried a hammer that produced bolts of lightning. Our day, Thursday, is named in Thor's honour.

◄ In Scandinavian mythology, Thor was the god of thunder.

▲ The Egyptian sun god, Re, was often shown with the head of a falcon.

376 **Hurricanes are named after a god.** The Mayan people lived in Central America, the part of the world that is most affected by hurricanes. Their creator god was called Huracan.

377
Totem poles honoured the Thunderbird. Certain tribes of Native American Indians built tall, painted totem poles, carved in the image of the Thunderbird. They wanted to keep the spirit happy, because they thought it brought rain to feed the plants.

▶ A Native American Indian totem pole depicting the spirit of the Thunderbird.

378
People once danced for rain. In hot places such as Africa, people developed dances to bring rain. These were performed by the village shaman (religious woman or man), using wooden instruments such as bullroarers. Sometimes water was sprinkled on the ground. Rain dances are still performed in some countries today.

◀ Shamans wore a special costume for their rain dance.

MAKE A BULLROARER

You will need:
wooden ruler   string

Ask an adult to drill a hole in one end of the ruler. Thread through the string, and knot it, to stop it slipping through the hole. In an open space, whirl the instrument above your head to create a wind noise!

Rain or shine?

▲ Kelp picks up any moisture in the air, so it is a good way of telling how damp the atmosphere is.

379 Seaweed can tell us if rain is on the way. Long ago, people looked to nature for clues about the weather. One traditional way of forecasting was to hang up strands of seaweed. If the seaweed stayed slimy, the air was damp and rain was likely. If the seaweed shrivelled up, the weather would be dry.

380 'Red sky at night is the sailor's delight'. This is one of the most famous pieces of weather lore and means that a glorious sunset is followed by a fine morning. The saying is also known as 'shepherd's delight'. There is no evidence that the saying is true, though.

I DON'T BELIEVE IT!

People used to say that cows lay down when rain was coming – but there is no truth in it! They lie down whether rain is on the way or not!

381 Groundhogs tell the weather when they wake. Of course, they don't really, but in parts of the USA, Groundhog Day is a huge celebration. On 2 February, people gather to see the groundhog come out. If you see the creature's shadow, it means there are six more weeks of cold to come.

Groundhog

▼ A blood—red sunset is delightful to look at, but it can't help a sailor to predict the next day's weather.

▲ The Moon is clearly visible in a cloudless night sky. Its light casts a silvery glow over the Earth.

382 'Clear moon, frost soon'. This old saying does have some truth in it. If there are few clouds in the sky, the view of the Moon will be clear – and there will also be no blanket of cloud to keep in the Earth's heat. That makes a frost more likely – during the colder months, at least.

383 The earliest weather records are over 3000 years old. They were found on a piece of tortoiseshell and had been written down by Chinese weather watchers. The inscriptions describe when it rained or snowed and how windy it was.

◄ Records of ancient weather were scratched on to this piece of shell.

Instruments and inventors

384 **The Tower of Winds was built 2000 years ago.** It was an eight-sided building and is the first known weather station. It had a wind vane on the roof and a water clock inside.

385 **The first barometer was made by one of Galileo's students.** Barometers measure air pressure. The first person to describe air pressure – and to make an instrument for measuring it – was an Italian, Evangelista Torricelli. He had studied under the great scientist Galileo. Torricelli made his barometer in 1643.

▲ This is how the Tower of Winds looks today. It was built by Andronicus of Cyrrhus in Athens around 75BC. Its eight sides face the points of the compass: north, northeast, east, southeast, south, southwest, west and northwest.

◀ Torricelli took a bowl of mercury and placed it under the open end of a glass tube, also filled with mercury. It was the weight, or pressure, of air on the mercury in the bowl that stopped the mercury in the tube from falling.

386 **Weather cocks have a special meaning.** They have four pointers that show the directions of north, south, east and west. The cockerel at the top swivels so that its head always shows the direction of the wind.

▶ Weather cocks are often placed on top of church steeples.

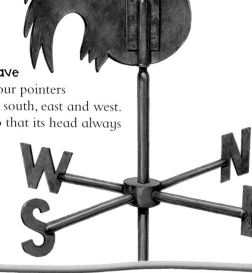

387
A weather house really can predict the weather. It is a type of hygrometer – an instrument that detects how much moisture is in the air. If there is lots, the rainy-day character comes out of the door!

▶ Weather houses have two figures. One comes out when the air is damp and the other when the air is dry.

◀ This early thermometer shows both the Fahrenheit and the Celsius temperature scales.

388
Fahrenheit made the first thermometer in 1714. Thermometers are instruments that measure temperature. Gabriel Daniel Fahrenheit invented the thermometer using a blob of mercury sealed in an airtight tube. The Fahrenheit scale for measuring heat was named after him. The Centigrade scale was introduced in 1742 by the Swedish scientist Anders Celsius.

QUIZ

1. What is another name for the liquid metal, mercury?

2. What does an anemometer measure?

3. What does a wind vane measure?

4. On the Fahrenheit scale, at what temperature does water freeze?

Answers:
1. Quicksilver 2. Wind speed
3. Wind direction 4. 32°F

169

World of weather

389 **Working out what the weather will be like is called forecasting.** By looking at changes in the atmosphere, and comparing them to weather patterns of the past, forecasters can make an accurate guess at what the weather will be tomorrow, the next day, or even further ahead than that. But even forecasters get it wrong sometimes!

390 **The first national weather offices appeared in the 1800s.** This was when people realized that science could explain how weather worked – and save people from disasters. The first network of weather stations was set up in France, in 1855. This was after the scientist Le Verrier showed how a French warship, sunk in a storm, could have been saved. Le Verrier explained how the path of the storm could have been tracked, and the ship sailed to safety.

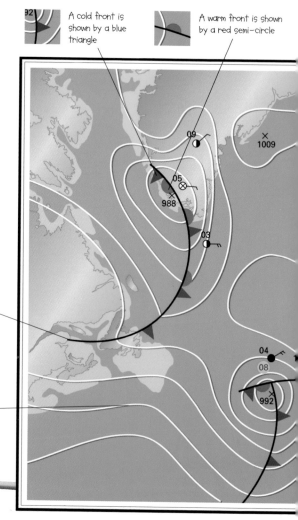

A cold front is shown by a blue triangle

A warm front is shown by a red semi-circle

Look for the black lines with red semi-circles and blue triangles – they represent an occluded front, where a cold front meets a warm front

These white lines are isobars – they connect places where air pressure is the same

WEATHER SYMBOLS

Learn how to represent the weather on your own synoptic charts. Here are some of the basic symbols to get you started. You may come across them in newspapers or while watching television. Can you guess what they mean?

391

Nations need to share weather data. By 1865, nearly 60 weather stations across Europe were swapping information. These early weather scientists, or meteorologists, realized that they needed to present their information using symbols that they could all understand. To this day, meteorologists plot their findings on maps called synoptic charts. They use lines called isobars to show which areas have the same air pressure. The Internet makes it easier for meteorologists to access information.

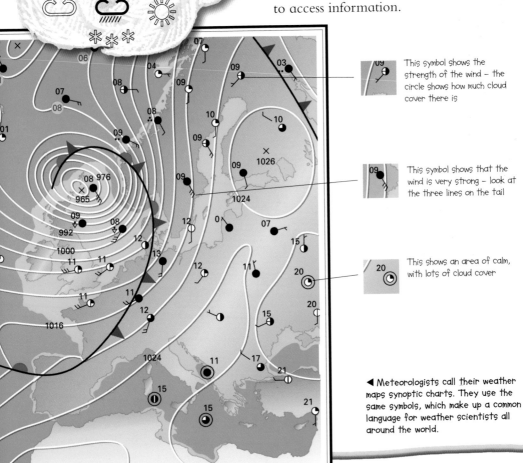

This symbol shows the strength of the wind – the circle shows how much cloud cover there is

This symbol shows that the wind is very strong – look at the three lines on the tail

This shows an area of calm, with lots of cloud cover

◀ Meteorologists call their weather maps synoptic charts. They use the same symbols, which make up a common language for weather scientists all around the world.

Weather watch

392 Balloons can tell us about the weather.

Weather balloons are hot-air balloons that are sent high into the atmosphere. As they rise, onboard equipment takes readings. These find out air pressure, and how moist, or humid, the air is, as well as how warm. The findings are radioed back to meteorologists on the ground, using a system called radiosonde. Hundreds of balloons are launched around the world every day.

▶ A weather balloon carries its scientific instruments high into the atmosphere.

393 Some planes hound the weather.

Weather planes provide more atmospheric measurements than balloons can. *Snoopy* is the name of one of the British weather planes. The instruments are carried on its long, pointy nose, so they can test the air ahead of the plane.

▼ *Snoopy's* long nose carries all the equipment needed to monitor the weather.

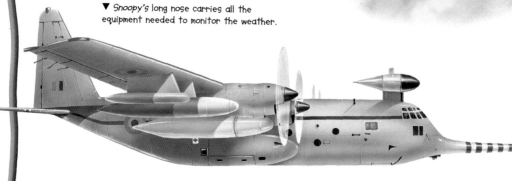

394

Satellites help save lives.
Their birds'-eye view of the Earth allows them to take amazing pictures of our weather systems. They can track hurricanes as they form over the oceans. Satellite-imaging has helped people to leave their homes and get out of a hurricane's path just in time.

I DON'T BELIEVE IT!

Some of the best weather photos have been taken by astronauts in space.

▲ A weather satellite takes photographs of Earth's weather systems from space.

► Currents carry the floating weather buoys around the oceans.

395

Some weather stations are all at sea. Weather buoys float on the surface of the oceans, measuring air pressure, temperature and wind direction. They are fitted with transmitters that beam information to satellites in space – which bounce the readings on to meteorologists. Tracking the buoys is just as important. They are carried along by ocean currents, which have a huge effect on our weather systems.

Changing climate

396 Climate change destroyed the dinosaurs – but no one can agree on what caused it. The best explanation is that a huge piece of space rock, called a meteorite, smashed into Earth. It threw up a giant cloud of dust that blocked out the Sun, plunging the world into cold and dark.

▼ Could a meteorite have crashed to Earth and changed the climate? A meteorite crater found in the Gulf of Mexico dates to 65 million years ago – exactly the time that the dinosaurs died out. Perhaps the impact changed the warm climate the dinosaurs were so used to.

397 Greenland used to be green! This island lies in the Arctic Ocean and is mostly covered by a huge ice sheet. Even in Viking times, Greenland was cold, but Viking settlers built at least two farming colonies there. These died out around the 1400s, after the climate cooled.

◄ Vikings settled on Greenland's coastline. Inland areas were covered in ice.

◄ Like all plants, rainforest trees take in carbon dioxide and give out oxygen. As rainforests are destroyed, the amount of carbon dioxide in the atmosphere increases.

398 A volcano can change the climate!

Big volcanic explosions can create dust that blots out the Sun, just as a meteorite impact can. Dust from the 1815 eruption of a volcano called Tambora did this. This made many crops fail around the world and many people starved.

399 Tree-felling is affecting our weather.

In areas of Southeast Asia and South America, rainforests are being cleared for farming. When the trees are burned, the fires release carbon dioxide – a greenhouse gas which helps to blanket the Earth and keep in the heat. Unfortunately, high levels of carbon dioxide raise the temperature too much.

400 Air temperatures are rising.

Scientists think the average world temperature may increase by around 1.5°C this century. This may not sound like much, but the extra warmth will mean more storms, including hurricanes and tornadoes, and more droughts too.

QUIZ

1. What may have caused the death of the dinosaurs?
2. Which settlers once lived along the coast of Greenland?
3. Which gas do plants take in?

Answers:
1. Meteorite impact 2. Vikings 3. Carbon dioxide

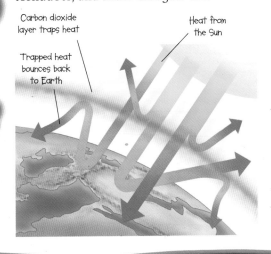

Carbon dioxide layer traps heat

Heat from the Sun

Trapped heat bounces back to Earth

► Too much carbon dioxide in the atmosphere creates a 'greenhouse effect'. Just as glass traps heat, so does carbon dioxide. This means more storms and droughts.